seasons & reasons TO CELEBRATE

When you're a quilter, you can dive into your fabric stash to enjoy your favorite season—at any time of the year! Tracy MacKay's seasonal wall hangings are fun to make with fusible appliqués of animals, flowers, and trees. There are eight quilted designs, including one that celebrates all twelve months. Several of these little quilts have a scattering of pieced blocks, while buttons and basic embroidery stitches add cheerful details. Choose your favorite design and stitch your own lighthearted creation. What a great way to use up your fabric scraps!

Tracy MacKay, aka Dandelion Mama

"I've been doing creative stuff like painting, sewing, and knitting since before I was born," says Tracy MacKay. "Well, maybe not that long. But close."

Tracy has attended the California Institute of the Arts and the Seattle Art Institute. While she is currently finishing a bachelor's degree in education and starting on a master's program in special education, she is also running a design business out of her home. All of this is taking place while Tracy raises her three much-loved children, which means that finding time to design—or even to sleep—can be tricky.

"When I get the chance," says Tracy, "I love going to thrift stores. I like finding wooden toys and old quilts. I also enjoy keeping a blog at dandelionmama.wordpress.com."

We're glad Tracy found the time to create these fun designs, and we think quilters everywhere will agree!

LEISURE ARTS, INC.
Little Rock, Arkansas

bee

quilt size: 44" x 44" (112 cm x 112 cm)

fabric requirements

Yardage is based on 43"/44" (109 cm/112 cm) wide fabric.

- $1^{1}/_{8}$ yds (1 m) **total** of assorted tan, cream, and beige prints for backgrounds
- $^{5}/_{8}$ yd (57 cm) of dark tan print for outer border
- $^{3}/_{8}$ yd (34 cm) of green print for middle border
- $^{3}/_{8}$ yd (34 cm) of green/black print for binding
- $^{1}/_{4}$ yd (23 cm) **each** of black and yellow prints for center and inner borders
- Assorted scrap fabrics for appliqués
- 3 yds (2.7 m) of fabric for backing

You will also need:

- 52" x 52" (132 cm x 132 cm) square of batting
- Black and green #8 pearl cotton
- Orange, green, pink, and blue embroidery floss
- Water-soluble fabric marking pen

industrious

cutting the pieces

Follow **Rotary Cutting**, *page 45, to cut fabric. Cut all strips across the selvage-to-selvage width of the fabric. Measurements given for* **background** *and* **center squares** *are exact. You may wish to cut these pieces 1" larger on all sides to allow for fraying and take up during appliqué and embroidery. Trim pieces to sizes given after all stitching is completed. All measurements include* $1/4$ *" seam allowances.*

From assorted tan, cream, and beige prints:
- Cut 12 **background squares** $8^1/2$" x $8^1/2$".
- Cut 4 **center squares** $7^1/2$" x $7^1/2$".

From dark tan print:
- Cut 2 **top/bottom outer borders** $3^1/2$" x $37^1/2$".
- Cut 2 **side outer borders** $3^1/2$" x $43^1/2$", pieced as necessary.

From green print:
- Cut 2 **top/bottom middle borders** 2" x $34^1/2$".
- Cut 2 **side middle borders** 2" x $37^1/2$".

From green/black print:
- Cut 5 **binding strips** $2^1/4$" wide.

From black print:
- Cut 4 **strips** $1^1/2$" wide.

From yellow print:
- Cut 4 **strips** $1^1/2$" wide.

cutting the appliqués

Follow **Fusible Appliqué**, *page 47, to use patterns on pages 8-11 and pattern insert.*

center
From assorted scrap fabrics:
- Cut 1 of *each* **wing**.
- Cut 1 of *each* **bee**.
- Cut 1 of *each* **hive section**.
- Cut 1 **stand**.
- Cut 1 **opening**.

january
From assorted scrap fabrics:
- Cut 1 **snowman**.
- Cut 1 of *each* star.
- Cut 1 **heart**.

february
From assorted scrap fabrics:
- Cut 1 of *each* **heart**.

march
From assorted scrap fabrics:
- Cut 1 of *each* **clover**.

april
From assorted scrap fabrics:
- Cut 1 **large egg**.
- Cut 1 **chick**.
- Cut 1 **wing**.
- Cut 1 **beak**.
- Cut 1 **small egg**.

may
From assorted scrap fabrics:
- Cut 1 of *each* **petal**.
- Cut 1 of *each* **center**.
- Cut 1 of *each* **stem**.
- Cut 1 of *each* **leaf**.

june
From assorted scrap fabrics:
- Cut 1 **inner rind**.
- Cut 1 **bud**.
- Cut 1 **watermelon**.
- Cut 1 **leaf**.
- Cut 1 **calyx**.
- Cut 1 **rind**.

july

From assorted scrap fabrics:

Note: Flag is cut from a stripe fabric.

- Cut 1 of *each* star.
- Cut 1 flag.
- Cut 1 field.

august

From assorted scrap fabrics:

- Cut 1 sunflower.
- Cut 1 stem/leaf.
- Cut 1 of *each* leaf.
- Cut 1 center.

september

From assorted scrap fabrics:

- Cut 1 of *each* apple.
- Cut 1 of *each* leaf.
- Cut 1 bucket.

october

From assorted scrap fabrics:

- Cut 1 leaf.
- Cut 1 stem.
- Cut 1 pumpkin.

november

From assorted scrap fabrics:

- Cut 1 beak.
- Cut 1 comb.
- Cut 1 wattle.
- Cut 1 body.
- Cut 1 of *each* wing.
- Cut 1 of *each* feather.

december

From assorted scrap fabrics:

- Cut 1 star.
- Cut 1 tree.
- Cut 1 trunk.

making the blocks

*Follow **Machine Piecing** and **Pressing**, page 46. Use a $1/4$" seam allowance. Refer to **Blanket Stitch Appliqué**, pages 48-49, for Hand or Machine Appliqué techniques. Refer to **Transferring Patterns**, page 49, to transfer embroidery details and **Hand Stitches**, pages 54-56, for embroidery stitches.*

1. Sew 4 center squares together to make center background. Arrange, fuse, and Blanket Stitch appliqué shapes to center background.
2. Transfer embroidery details to center background. Use black pearl cotton to work Running Stitch bee trails, Backstitch the words, and make Straight Stitch antennae with French Knot ends.
3. Arrange, fuse, and Blanket Stitch appliqué shapes for each month to a background square to make 12 month blocks.
4. Transfer embroidery details to month blocks. Use black pearl cotton to Backstitch the month names and any other words. Add the following details to the month blocks:

   - january – Work French Knot eyes and mouth with black pearl cotton. Work Satin Stitch nose with 2 strands of orange floss. Work Backstitch branches and snow with black pearl cotton. Straight Stitch around the heart with black pearl cotton.
   - march –Work Backstitch stems and Straight Stitch grass using black pearl cotton.

- **april** – Work Backstitch legs with 3 strands of orange floss. Work French Knot eye using black pearl cotton.
- **june** – Work Backstitch stem using black pearl cotton.
- **july** –Work Running Stitch fireworks using 1 strand of blue, pink, green, or orange floss. Work Stem Stitch hills using green pearl cotton. Work a Backstitch flagpole using black pearl cotton.
- **september** – Work Straight Stitch stems using green pearl cotton.
- **october** – Work a Backstitch tendril using black pearl cotton.
- **november** – Work a French Knot eye and Backstitch legs using black pearl cotton.

assembling the quilt top

1. For center borders, alternate colors and sew 4 black print strips and 4 yellow print strips together to make **Strip Set**. Cut across Strip Set at 1¹/₂" intervals to make **Unit 1**. Make 24 Unit 1's.

Strip Set (make 1)   **Unit 1** (make 24)

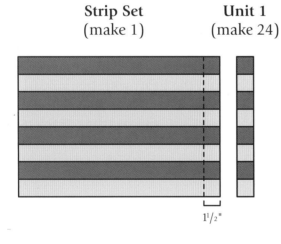

1¹/₂"

2. Sew 2 Unit 1's together to make **center border**. Make 4 center borders.

Center Border (make 4)

3. Remove 2 squares from 2 center borders (14 squares remaining). Sew 1 of these to the top and bottom of center background. Sew 1 remaining center border to each side of center background to complete **center**.

Center

4. Sew 4 Unit 1's together to make **inner border**. Make 4 inner borders. Add the squares removed from the center borders to the ends of 2 inner borders (34 squares total) to make 2 **side inner borders**. Remaining 2 inner borders are **top/bottom inner borders**. Set all inner borders aside.

Inner borders (make 4)

5. Sew **January**, **February**, **March**, and **April** blocks together to make **Row 1**.

Row 1

6. Sew **December** and **November** blocks together. Sew **May** and **June** blocks together. Sew December/November blocks to left side and May/June blocks to right side of Center to make **Row 2**.

Row 2

7. Sew **October**, **September**, **August**, and **July** together to complete **Row 3**.

Row 3

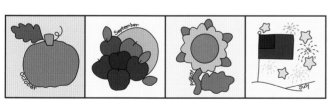

8. Sew Row 1, Row 2, and Row 3 together to complete **quilt top center**.

Quilt Top Center

9. Sew 1 **top/bottom inner border** to the top and bottom of quilt top center. Sew 1 **side inner border** to each side of the quilt top center.

10. Matching centers and corners, sew **top/bottom middle borders** then **side middle borders** to quilt top center. Matching centers and corners, sew **top/bottom outer borders** and then **side outer borders** to quilt top center to complete **quilt top**.

completing the quilt

1. Follow **Quilting**, page 50, to mark, layer, and quilt as desired. Our quilt is hand quilted with a Running Stitch outlining all blocks and appliqués.

2. If desired, follow **Adding A Hanging Sleeve**, page 52, to add a hanging sleeve.

3. Follow **Binding**, page 52, to bind quilt using **binding strips**.

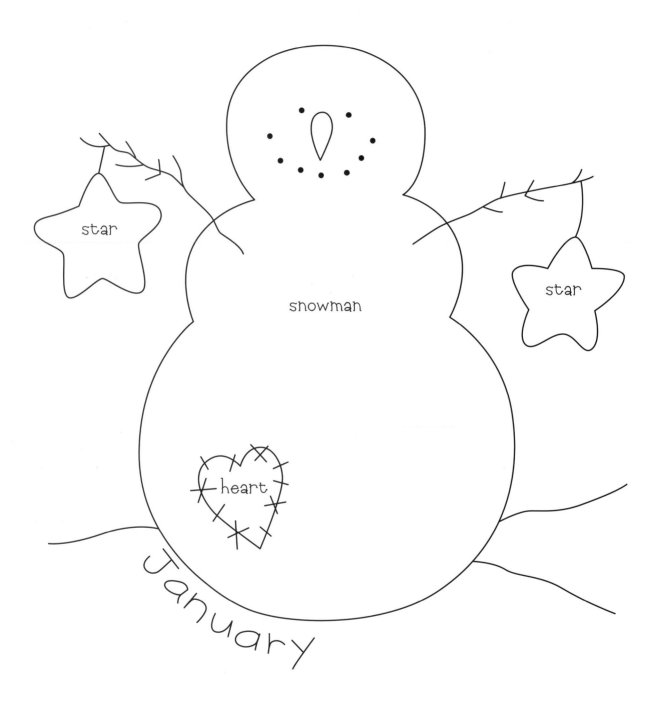

star

star

snowman

heart

January

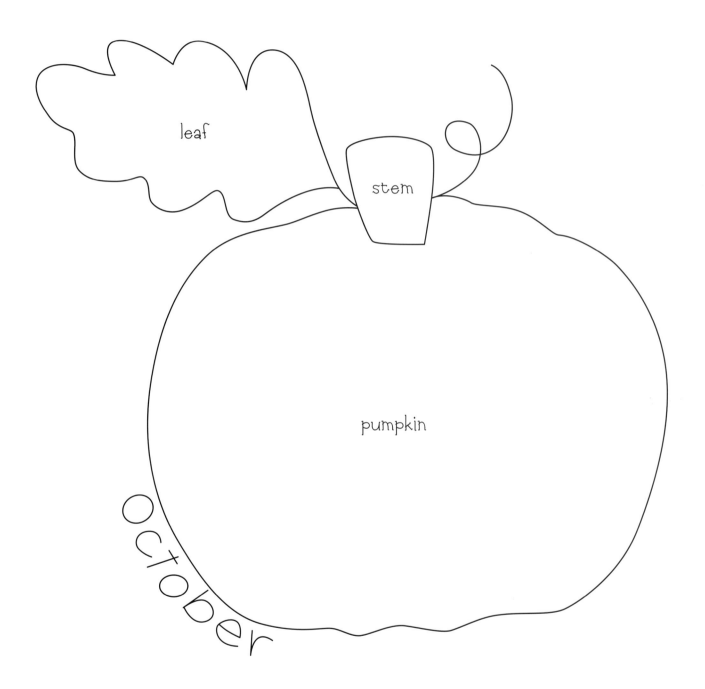

leaf

stem

pumpkin

october

9

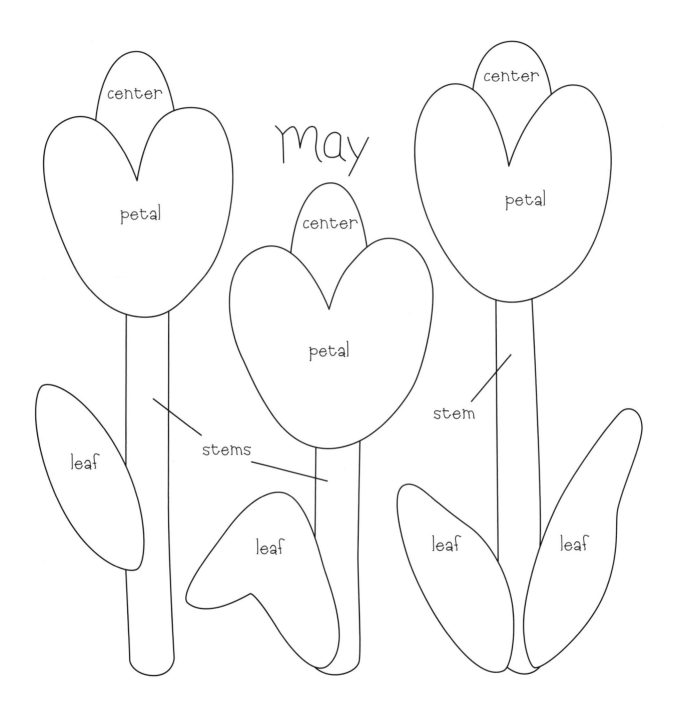

center

petal

may

center

petal

center

petal

stem

leaf

stems

leaf

leaf

leaf

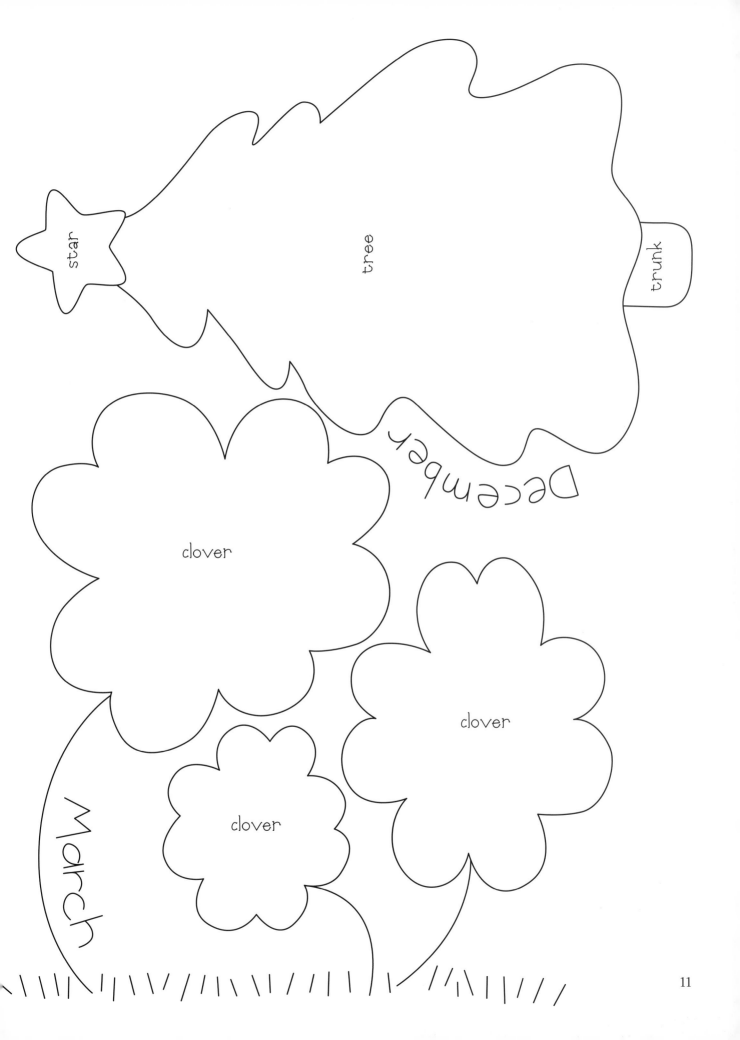

star

tree

trunk

December

clover

clover

clover

March

11

let it snow banner

quilt size: 23^1/$_2$" x 43" (60 cm x 109 cm)

fabric requirements

Yardage is based on 43"/44" (109 cm/112 cm) wide fabric. **Note:** *A fat quarter measures approximately 18" x 22" (46 cm x 56 cm).*

   ^{1}/$_2$ yd (46 cm) of light blue print for background
   ^{3}/$_8$ yd (34 cm) of blue dot for outer border
   ^{3}/$_8$ yd (34 cm) of blue print for binding
   ^{1}/$_4$ yd (23 cm) of red stripe for inner border
   1 fat quarter of red print for tabs
   ^{1}/$_4$ yd (23 cm) of white flannel for snowmen
   Assorted scrap fabrics for scarves and noses
   1^1/$_2$ yds (1.4 m) of fabric for backing
You will also need:
   31" x 51" (79 cm x 130 cm) rectangle of batting
   Black #8 pearl cotton
   Brown embroidery floss
   3 white 1" (25 mm) dia. star buttons
   Red crayon

cutting the pieces

*Follow **Rotary Cutting**, page 45, to cut fabric. Cut strips across the selvage-to-selvage width of the fabric unless otherwise noted. Measurements given for **background** are exact. You may wish to cut this piece 1" larger on all sides to allow for fraying and take up during appliqué and embroidery. Trim piece to size given after all stitching is completed. All measurements include ¹/₄" seam allowances. Inner and outer borders are cut longer than needed and will be trimmed during construction.*

From light blue print:
- Cut 1 **background** 16" x 35".

From blue dot:
- Cut 2 **side outer borders** 2³/₄" x 34".
- Cut 1 **top outer border** 2³/₄" x 23".
- Cut 2 **bottom outer borders** 2³/₄" x 17".

From blue print:
- Cut 4 **binding strips** 2¹/₄" wide.

From red stripe fabric:
- Cut 2 **side inner borders** 1³/₄" x 32".
- Cut 1 **top inner border** 1³/₄" x 18¹/₂".
- Cut 2 **bottom inner borders** 1³/₄" x 14".

From red print fat quarter:
- Cut 3 **rectangles** 5" x 9¹/₂".

cutting the appliqués

*Follow **Fusible Appliqué**, page 47, to use patterns on pattern inserts. **Note:** Snowmen are cut as 1 piece. Grey lines on pattern are Blanket Stitch lines.*

From white flannel:
- Cut **snowmen**.

From assorted scrap fabrics:
- Cut 1 of *each* **scarf**.
- Cut 1 of *each* **nose**.

making the quilt top

*Follow **Machine Piecing** and **Pressing**, page 46. Use a ¹/₄" seam allowance. Refer to **Blanket Stitch Appliqué**, pages 48-49, for Hand or Machine Appliqué techniques. Refer to **Transferring Patterns**, page 49, to transfer embroidery details and **Hand Stitches**, pages 54-56, for embroidery stitches.*

1. Referring to **Figs. 1** and **2**, fold **background** in half lengthwise with right sides facing; mark 5¹/₄" from bottom. Align rotary cutting ruler with this mark and with the fold; cut to make banner point.

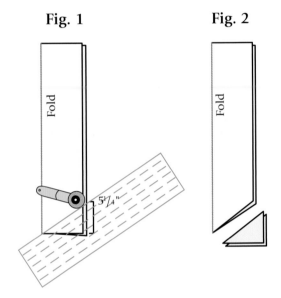

Fig. 1   **Fig. 2**

2. Arrange, fuse, and Blanket Stitch **appliqué shapes** to background. Transfer embroidery details to snowmen and words to background. Work French Knot eyes and smiles and Backstitch wording with black pearl cotton. Work Chain Stitch arms using 2 strands of brown embroidery floss. To add color to cheeks, rub crayon on a soft cloth and then lightly rub cloth on cheeks.

3. Sew **side inner borders** to background. Following angle of the point of background, trim borders (**Fig. 3**).

Fig. 3

4. Sew 1 **bottom inner border** to right side of bottom edge of background; trim (**Fig. 4**). Sew remaining bottom inner border to left side; trim (**Fig. 5**).

Fig. 4   **Fig. 5**

5. Matching centers and corners, sew **top inner border** to top edge of background to complete **quilt top center**.
6. Repeat Steps 3-5 with using **outer borders** to complete **Quilt Top**.

completing the quilt

1. Follow **Quilting**, page 50, to mark, layer, and quilt as desired. Our quilt is hand quilted with a Running Stitch outlining the background and snowmen.
2. Follow **Binding**, page 52, to bind quilt using **binding strips**.
3. For **tabs**, follow **Fig. 6** to draw cutting lines on wrong side of 3 **rectangles**. Matching right sides, pin 1 marked and 1 unmarked rectangle together. Leaving top edge open for turning sew rectangles together; trim on cutting lines (**Fig. 7**). Turn right side out; press. Make 3 tabs.

Fig. 6

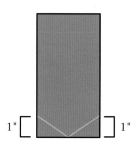

Fig. 7

4. Evenly space pointed ends of tabs across top edge of quilt front; pin. Sewing through all layers, sew 1 white star button to each tab. Turning under raw edges, blindstitch short straight edges of tabs to quilt back just below binding.

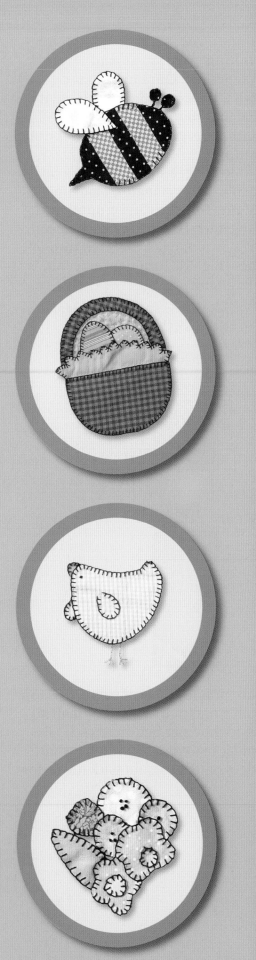

the march

quilt size: 37" x 34" (94 cm x 86 cm)

fabric requirements

*Yardage is based on 43"/44" (109 cm/112 cm) wide fabric. **Note**: A fat quarter measures approximately 18" x 22" (46 cm x 56 cm) and a fat eighth measures approximately 11" x 18" (28 cm x 46 cm).*

- 1 fat quarter *each* of 8 assorted tan prints for appliqué backgrounds and star blocks
- 1 fat eighth of tan print for fence and checkerboard unit
- 1 fat eighth *each* of 8 assorted pastel prints for star blocks, checkerboard unit, and corner squares
- $1/8$ yd (11 cm) of dark brown print for fence
- $3/8$ yd (34 cm) of light green stripe for grass strip and binding
- $1/4$ yd (23 cm) of dark green print for inner border
- $1/2$ yd (46 cm) of pink stripe for outer border
- 1 fat quarter of cream print for hare
- Assorted scrap fabrics for appliqués
- 1 fat eighth *each* of 2 gold/brown prints for baskets
- 4" x 4" (10 cm x 10 cm) square of white flannel or batting for hare tail
- $1^{1}/4$ yds (1.1 m) of fabric for backing

You will also need:
- 45" x 42" (114 cm x 107 cm) rectangle of batting
- Black #8 pearl cotton
- Orange embroidery floss
- 1 ladybug button

cutting the pieces

*Follow **Rotary Cutting**, page 45, to cut fabric. Cut border strips across the selvage-to-selvage width of the fabric. Measurements given for **backgrounds** and **welcome spring strip** are exact. You may wish to cut these pieces 1" larger on all sides to allow for fraying and take up during appliqué and embroidery. Trim pieces to sizes given after all stitching is completed. All measurements include $1/4$" seam allowances.*

- Cut 1 **hare background** 11" x 15".
- Cut 1 **flower basket background** 11" x $10^1/2$".
- Cut 1 **egg basket background** $7^1/2$" x $8^1/2$".
- Cut 1 **bumblebee background** $5^3/4$" x 5".
- Cut 1 **chick background** $5^3/4$" x 5".
- Cut 4 *sets* of 4 **small squares** 2" x 2" and 4 **rectangles** 2" x $3^1/2$".

- Cut 1 **welcome spring strip** 3" x $14^1/2$".
- Cut 1 **fence strip A** 13" x $1^1/4$".
- Cut 1 **fence strip B** 13" x 1".
- Cut 1 **fence strip C** 13" x $1^1/2$".
- Cut 7 **checkerboard squares** 2" x 2".

- Cut 4 *sets* of 8 **small squares** 2" x 2".
- Cut 4 assorted **large squares** $3^1/2$" x $3^1/2$".
- Cut 1 *set* of 4 **corner squares** $3^1/2$" x $3^1/2$".
- Cut 7 **checkerboard squares** 2" x 2".

- Cut 2 **fence rails** 13" x $1^1/4$".
- Cut 5 **fence pickets** $4^1/4$" x $1^1/2$".

- Cut 1 **grass strip** $2^1/4$" x $14^1/2$".
- Cut 4 **binding strips** $2^1/4$" wide.

- Cut 2 **side inner borders** 2" x $24^1/2$".
- Cut 2 **top/bottom inner borders** 2" x $30^1/2$".

- Cut 2 **side outer borders** $3^1/2$" x $27^1/2$".
- Cut 2 **top/bottom outer borders** $3^1/2$" x $30^1/2$".

cutting the appliqués

*Follow **Fusible Appliqué**, page 47, to use patterns on page 23 and pattern insert. **Note:** Grey lines on hare and chick patterns are Blanket Stitch lines. Do not cut on these lines.*

- Cut 1 **hare**.

- Cut 1 of *each* **petal**.
- Cut 1 of *each* **circle**.
- Cut 1 of *each* **heart**.
- Cut 1 of *each* **leaf**.
- Cut 1 of *each* **center**.
- Cut 1 of *each* **wing**.
- Cut 1 **bee**.
- Cut 1 of *each* **antennae**.
- Cut 1 of *each* **stripe**.
- Cut 1 **chick**.
- Cut 1 **beak**.
- Cut 1 **small egg**.
- Cut 1 **large egg**.
- Cut 1 **grass**.

- Cut 1 **flower basket** and 1 **flower basket handle**.
- Cut 1 **egg basket** and 1 **egg basket handle**.

- Cut 1 **tail**.

making the blocks and units

*Follow **Machine Piecing** and **Pressing**, page 46. Use a ¹/₄" seam allowance. Refer to **Blanket Stitch Appliqué**, pages 48-49, for Hand or Machine Appliqué techniques. Refer to **Transferring Patterns**, page 49, to transfer embroidery details and **Hand Stitches**, pages 54-56, for embroidery stitches.*

appliqué blocks

1. To make **Flower Basket Block**, arrange, fuse, and Blanket Stitch **appliqué shapes** to **flower basket background**. Transfer embroidery details to background. Using black pearl cotton, work Chain Stitches to complete basket handle and 3 or 4 French Knots on each circle.

Flower Basket Block A

2. To make **Bumblebee Block**, arrange, fuse, and Blanket Stitch **appliqué shapes** to **bumblebee background**. To connect antennae ends to bee, work Straight Stitches with black pearl cotton.

Bumblebee Block

3. To make **Chick Block**, arrange, fuse, and Blanket Stitch **appliqué shapes** to **chick background**. Work a French Knot eye with black pearl cotton. Work Backstitch legs using 2 strands of orange floss. Transfer wing embroidery detail from chick pattern and work Blanket Stitch detail using black pearl cotton. **Note:** If Machine Blanket Stitching appliqués, work wing detail with a Machine Blanket Stitch.

Chick Block

4. To make **Hare Block**, arrange, fuse, and Blanket Stitch **appliqué shapes** to **hare background**. Transfer eye, ear, and leg embroidery details from hare pattern. Work a Backstitch eye using black pearl cotton. Work Blanket Stitch ear and leg details using black pearl cotton or a Machine Blanket Stitch. To add color to cheeks, rub crayon on a soft cloth and then lightly rub cloth on cheeks.

Hare Block

5. To make **Egg Basket Block**, arrange, fuse, and Blanket Stitch **appliqué shapes** to **egg basket background**.

Egg Basket Block

rail fence block

1. Matching long edges and alternating colors, sew tan **fence strip A,** 1 dark brown **fence rail,** 1 tan **fence strip B,** 1 dark brown **fence rail,** and 1 wide tan **fence strip C** together to make **Strip Set.** Cut across Strip Set at 2" intervals to make **Unit 1.** Make 6 Unit 1's.

Strip Set (make 1)	**Unit 1** (make 6)

2"

2. Matching long edges, sew 6 Unit 1's and 5 **fence pickets** together to make **Unit 2.**

Unit 2

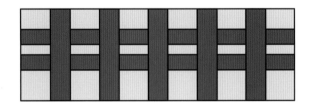

3. Sew **welcome spring strip** to top edge and **grass strip** to the bottom edge of Unit 2.
4. Transfer embroidery details to welcome spring strip. Work Running Stitch wording using black pearl cotton.

Rail Fence Block

sawtooth star block

For each Sawtooth Star Block you will need 1 set of 4 tan rectangles and 4 tan small squares and 1 set of 8 pastel small squares and 1 pastel large square.

1. Place 1 pastel **small square** on one corner of 1 tan **rectangle** and stitch diagonally. Trim $1/4$" from stitching line (**Fig. 1**). Press open (**Fig. 2**).

Fig. 1	**Fig. 2**

2. Repeat Step 1 to add 1 pastel small square to opposite end of tan rectangle (**Fig. 3**) to complete **Flying Geese Unit.** Make 4 Flying Geese Units.

Fig. 3

Flying Geese Unit (make 4)

3. Sew 1 tan **small square** to each end of 1 Flying Geese Unit to make **Unit 3**. Make 2 Unit 3's.

Unit 3 (make 2)

4. Sew 1 Flying Geese Unit to each side of **pastel large square** to make **Unit 4**.

Unit 4 (make 1)

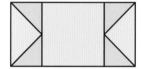

5. Sew 1 Unit 3 to top and the bottom of Unit 4 to make **Sawtooth Star Block**. Make 4 Sawtooth Star Blocks.

Sawtooth Star Block (make 4)

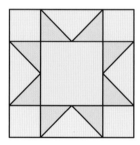

checkerboard unit

1. Alternating colors, sew 7 pastel **checkerboard squares** and 7 tan **checkerboard squares** together to make **Checkerboard Unit**.

Checkerboard Unit

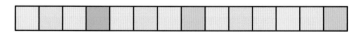

assembling the quilt top

Refer to Quilt Top Center Diagram, page 22, for placement.

1. Sew **Flower Basket Block, Bumblee Block,** and **Chick Block** together to make **Unit 5**.

Unit 5

2. Sew **Hare Block** to the right side of Unit 5 to make **Unit 6**.

Unit 6

3. Sew **Checkerboard Unit** to the top edge of Unit 6 to make **Unit 7**.

Unit 7

4. Sew **Rail Fence Block** and **Egg Basket Block** together to make **Unit 8**.

Unit 8

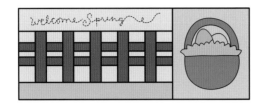

5. Sew **Units 7** and **Unit 8** together to make **Unit 9**.

Unit 9

6. Sew 4 **Sawtooth Star Blocks** together to make **Unit 10**. Sew Unit 10 to right side of Unit 9 to complete **quilt top center**.

Unit 10

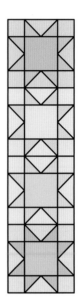

Quilt Top Center

7. Matching centers and corners, sew **side inner borders** to quilt top center, then add **top/ bottom inner borders**.

8. Matching centers and corners, sew **side outer borders** to quilt top center. Sew a **pastel large square** to each end of each **top/ bottom outer border**. Sew top/bottom outer borders to quilt top center.

completing the quilt

1. Follow **Quilting**, page 50, to mark, layer, and quilt as desired. Our quilt is hand quilted with a Running Stitch outlining the blocks and large appliqué shapes.
2. If desired, follow **Adding a Hanging Sleeve**, page 52, to add a hanging sleeve.
3. Follow **Binding**, page 52, to bind quilt using **binding strips**.
4. Stitching through all layers, sew ladybug button to welcome spring strip.

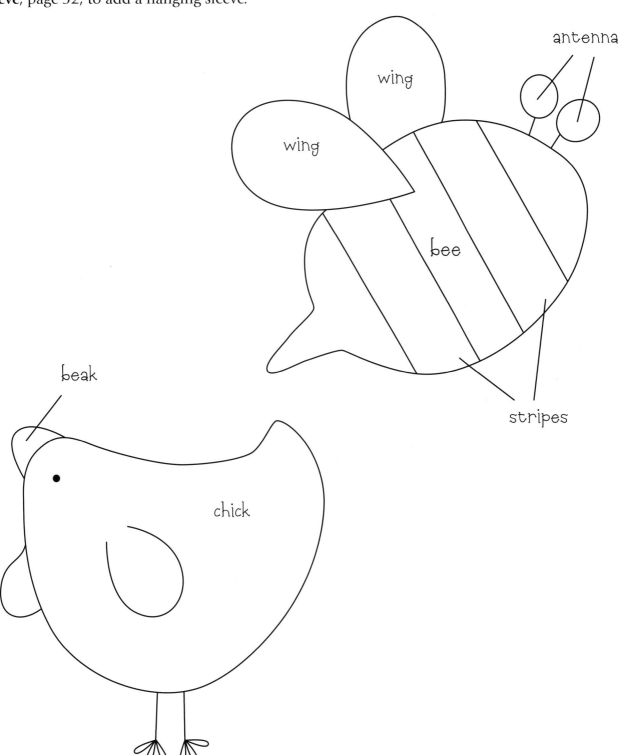

america the beautiful

quilt size: 24¹/₂" x 50" (62 cm x 127 cm)

fabric requirements

Yardage is based on 43"/44" (109 cm/112 cm) wide fabric. **Note:** *A fat quarter measures approximately 18" x 22" (46 cm x 56 cm) and a fat eighth measures approximately 11" x 18" (28 cm x 46 cm).*

- 1 fat quarter *each* of 2 gold prints for sun rays
- 1 fat quarter of white print for sun rays
- 6" x 6¹/₂" (15 x 17 cm) rectangle of blue print for flag field
- 1 fat quarter *each* of red print and beige print for flag, grey print for sky, and blue batik for sea and clouds
- 1 fat eighth *each* of 4 purple prints for mountains
- 1 fat eighth *each* of 2 orange prints for hills
- 1 fat eighth *each* of 5 green prints for hills and trees
- Assorted scrap fabrics for sun, tree trunks, and river
- ³/₄ yd (69 cm) of dark blue print for borders
- ³/₈ yd (34 cm) of striped fabric for binding
- 1⁵/₈ yds (1.5 m) of fabric for backing

You will also need:

- 32¹/₂" x 58" (83 cm x 147 cm) rectangle of batting
- Black #8 pearl cotton
- 9 gold ⁵/₈" (16 mm) star buttons
- Fabric glue stick (optional)

THIS LAND SHALL BE

A LAND OF LIBERTY...

FROM SEA TO SHINING SEA!

cutting the pieces

Follow **Rotary Cutting**, *page 45, to cut fabric. Cut all strips across the selvage-to-selvage width of the fabric. All measurements include* ¹/₄" *seam allowances.*

From 1 gold print fat quarter:
- Cut 2 **sun rays** 4¹/₂" x 12".

From remaining gold print fat quarter:
- Cut 4 **sun rays** 4¹/₂" x 12".

From white print fat eighth:
- Cut 4 **sun rays** 4¹/₂" x 12".

From red print fat quarter:
- Cut 2 **short strips** 2" x 11".
- Cut 2 **long strips** 2" x 16¹/₂".

From beige print fat quarter:
- Cut 2 **short strips** 2" x 11".
- Cut 1 **long strip** 2" x 16¹/₂".

From grey print fat quarter:
- Cut 1 **background** 16¹/₂" x 16".

From blue batik fat quarter:
- Cut 1 **sea** 16¹/₂" x 8¹/₂".

From dark blue print fabric:
- Cut 2 **top/bottom borders** 4¹/₄" x 24".
- Cut 2 **side borders** 4¹/₄" x 42", pieced as necessary.

From striped fabric:
- Cut 5 **binding strips** 2¹/₄" wide.

cutting the appliqués

Follow **Fusible Appliqué**, *page 47, to use patterns on page 29 and pattern inserts.*

From blue batik:
- Cut 1 of *each* **cloud**.

From purple print fat eighths:
- Cut 1 of *each* **mountain**.

From orange print fat eighths:
- Cut 1 of *each* **hill** (**A** and **B**).

From green print fat eighths:
- Cut 1 of *each* **hill** (**C** and **D**).
- Cut 1 of *each* **tree**.

From assorted scrap fabrics:
- Cut 1 **sun**.
- Cut 1 **river**.
- Cut 1 of *each* **tree trunk**.

making the blocks

Follow **Machine Piecing** and **Pressing**, *page 46. Use a* ¹/₄" *seam allowance. Refer to* **Blanket Stitch Appliqué**, *pages 48-49, for Hand or Machine Appliqué techniques. Refer to* **Transferring Patterns**, *page 49, to transfer embroidery details and* **Hand Stitches**, *pages 54-56, for embroidery stitches.*

sun block

Paper piecing patterns **A** *and* **B** *are on pattern insert. Trace or photocopy each pattern once to make foundations A and B. Always use a dry iron when pressing. Some photocopied patterns may smear when ironed. Test your patterns and use a pressing cloth if needed. Set stitch length to 18 stitches per inch to make paper removal easier. Always stitch with the printed side of the paper foundation facing up.*

1. Matching wrong side of fabric to unprinted side of paper, cover area 1 of foundation A with 1 gold **sun ray**. Pin or use a small dab from a glue stick to hold fabric in place (**Fig. 1**).

Fig. 1

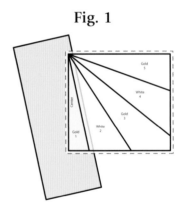

2. Turn foundation A over. Matching right sides of fabric and having at least ¹/₄" of fabric extending into area 2, pin 1 white sun ray over area 1 and gold sun ray (**Fig. 2**).

Fig. 2

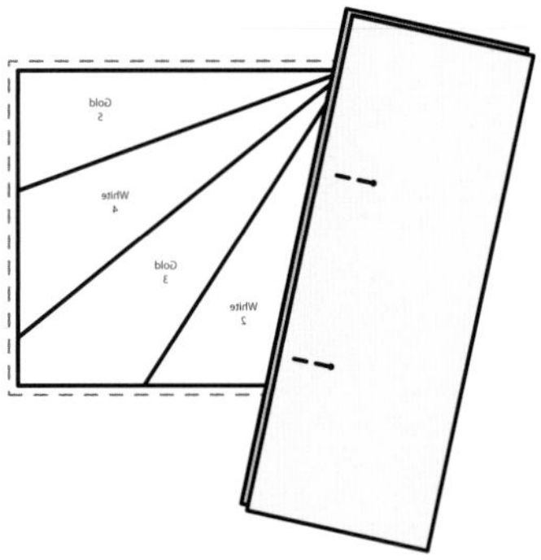

With right side of foundation A facing up, sew along line between areas 1 and 2, extending seam a few stitches beyond beginning and ending of line (**Fig. 3**).

Fig. 3

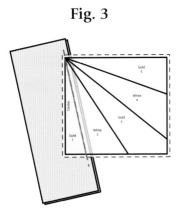

Fold foundation A back on stitched line and trim seam allowances to $^1/_4$" (**Fig. 4**).

Fig. 4

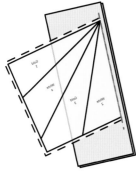

Open area 2 sun ray, press (**Fig. 5**), and pin to foundation A.

Fig. 5

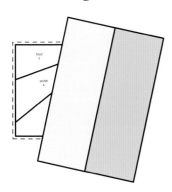

6. Continue adding sun rays, alternating gold and white fabrics (**Fig. 6**), until all areas of foundation A are covered.

Fig. 6

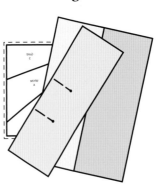

7. Trim fabric and foundation A along outer dashed lines to complete **Unit 1**. Repeat Steps 1-6 using foundation B to make **Unit 2**.

Unit 1   **Unit 2**

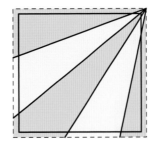
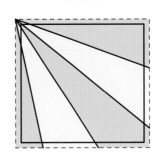

8. Matching right sides and center seamlines, insert an alignment pin straight through the corners of Units 1 and 2 (**Fig. 7**). Pin Units together then remove alignment pins. Stitch on center seamline, extending stitches to raw edges (**Fig. 8**). Carefully remove paper; press seam allowances open to complete **Sun Ray Background**.

Fig. 7   **Fig. 8**

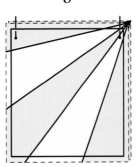
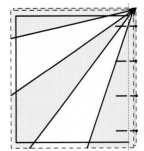

Sun Ray Background

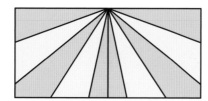

9. Matching outer straight edges of appliqué shapes with edges of background, arrange, fuse, and Blanket Stitch **sun** and **clouds** to Sun Ray Background to complete **Sun Block**.

Sun Block

flag block

1. Alternating red and beige, sew 4 **short strips** together to make **Unit 3**.

Unit 3

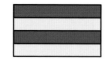

2. Sew **flag field** to left edge of Unit 3 to make **Unit 4**.

Unit 4

3. Alternating red and beige, sew **long strips** together to make **Unit 5**.

Unit 5

4. Sew Unit 4 and Unit 5 together to complete **Flag Background**.

Flag Background

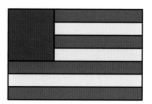

5. Transfer words to flag background. Work Backstitch words and French Knot details using black pearl cotton.
6. Use black pearl cotton to sew gold star buttons to flag field to complete **Flag Block**.

Flag Block

landscape block

1. Matching outer straight edges of appliqué shapes with edges of background, arrange, fuse, and Blanket Stitch **mountains**, **hills (A-D)**, and **river** to **background**.
2. Catching bottom edges of appliqué shapes in the seam allowance, sew **sea** to bottom edge of background to complete **Landscape Block**.

Landscape Block

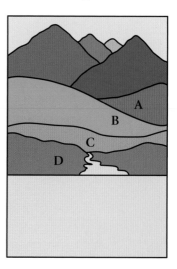

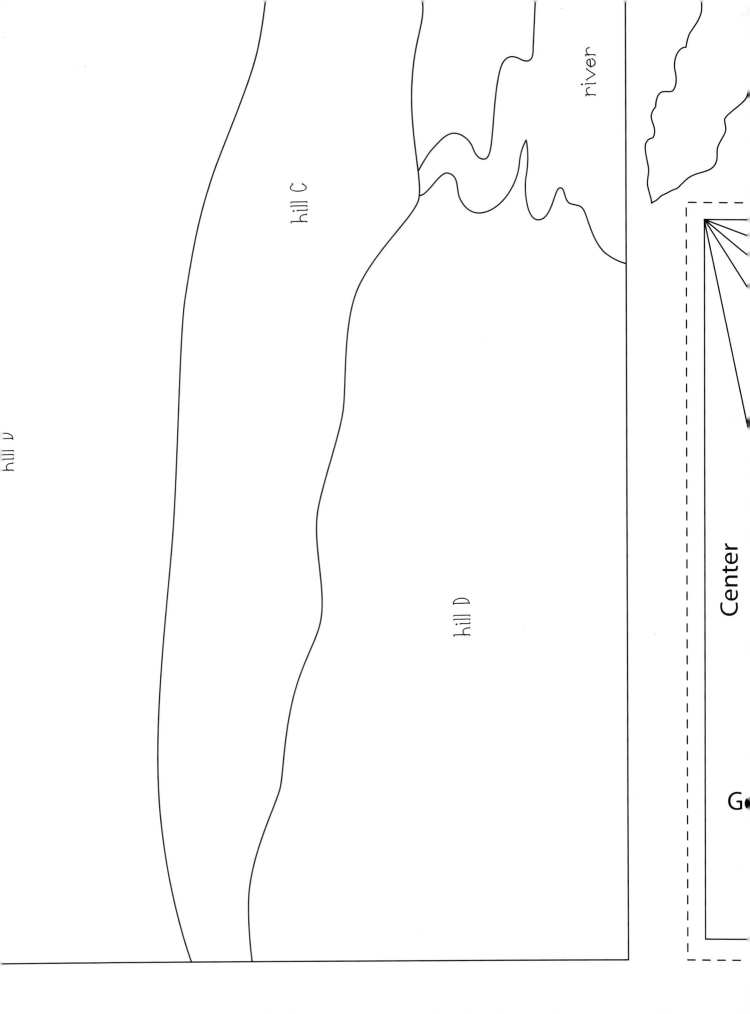

hill D

hill C

river

hill D

Center

G

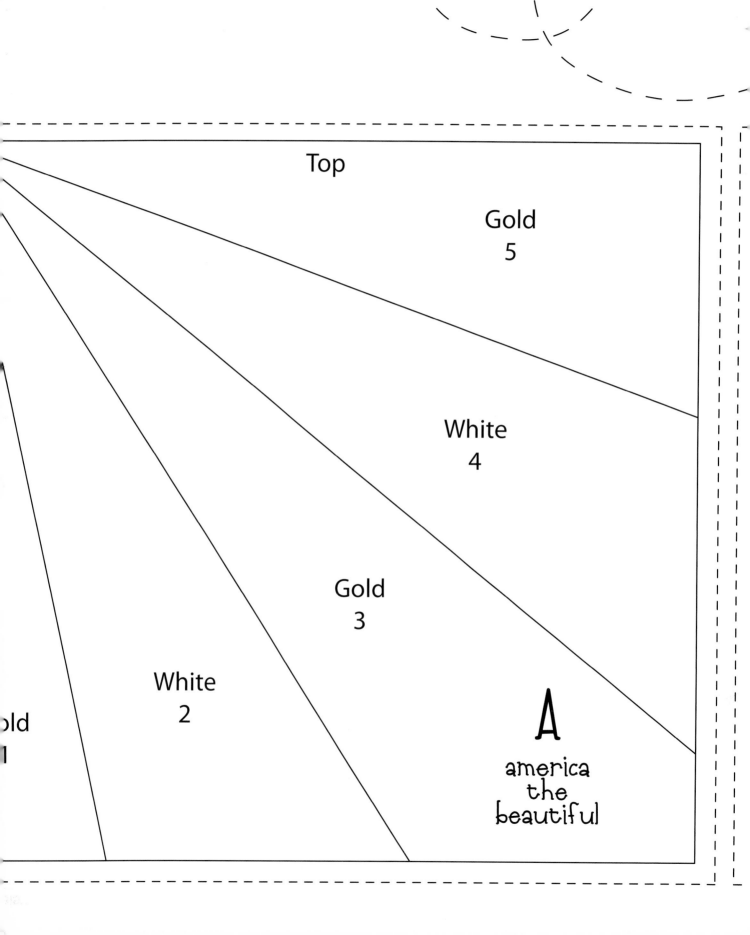

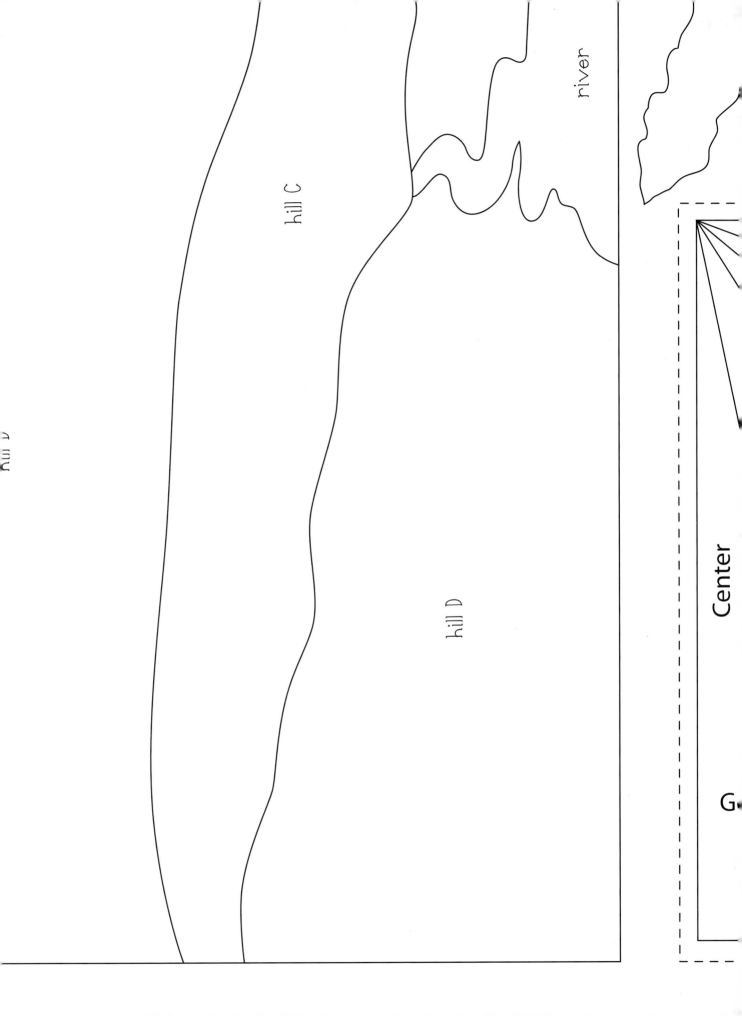

hill C

hill D

river

hill B

Center

G

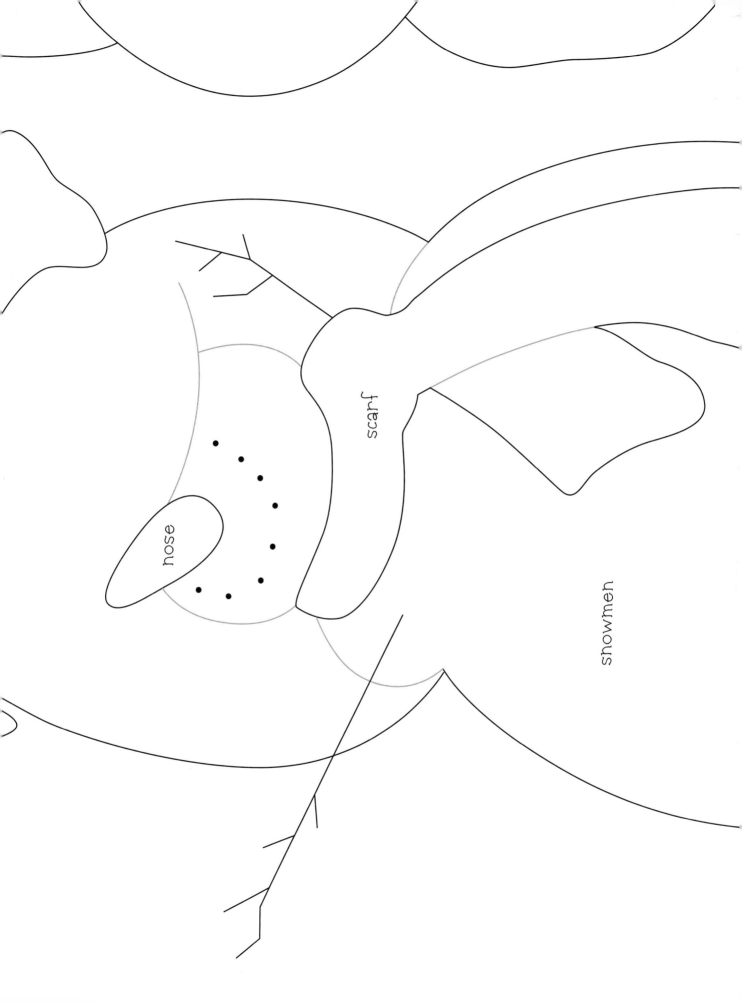

nose

scarf

showmen

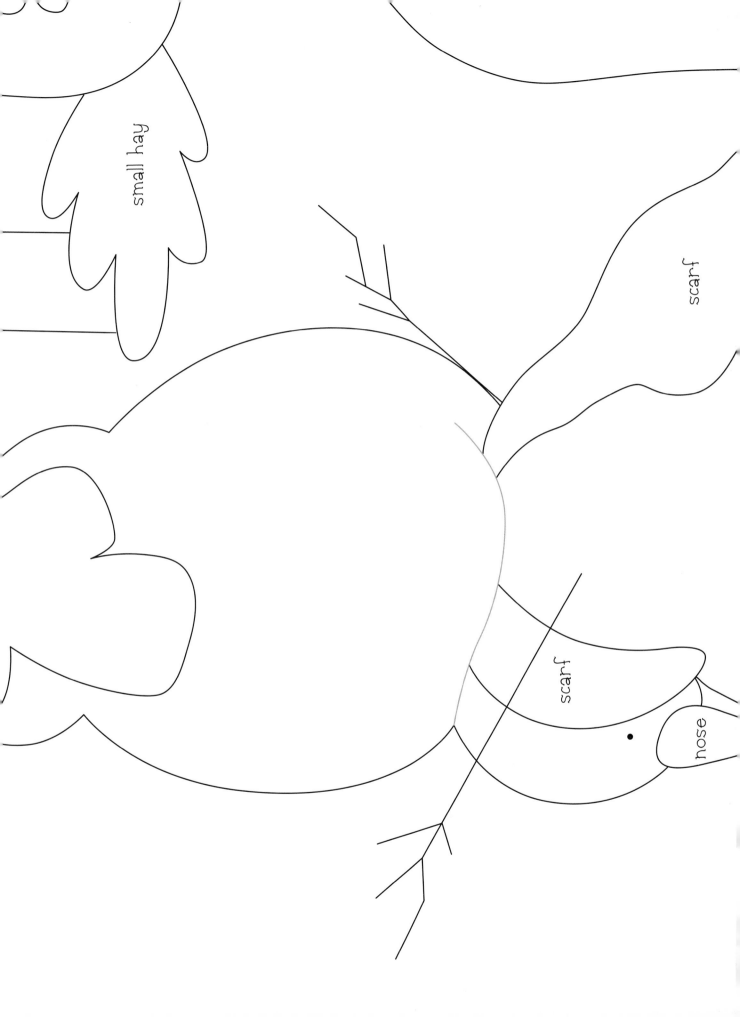

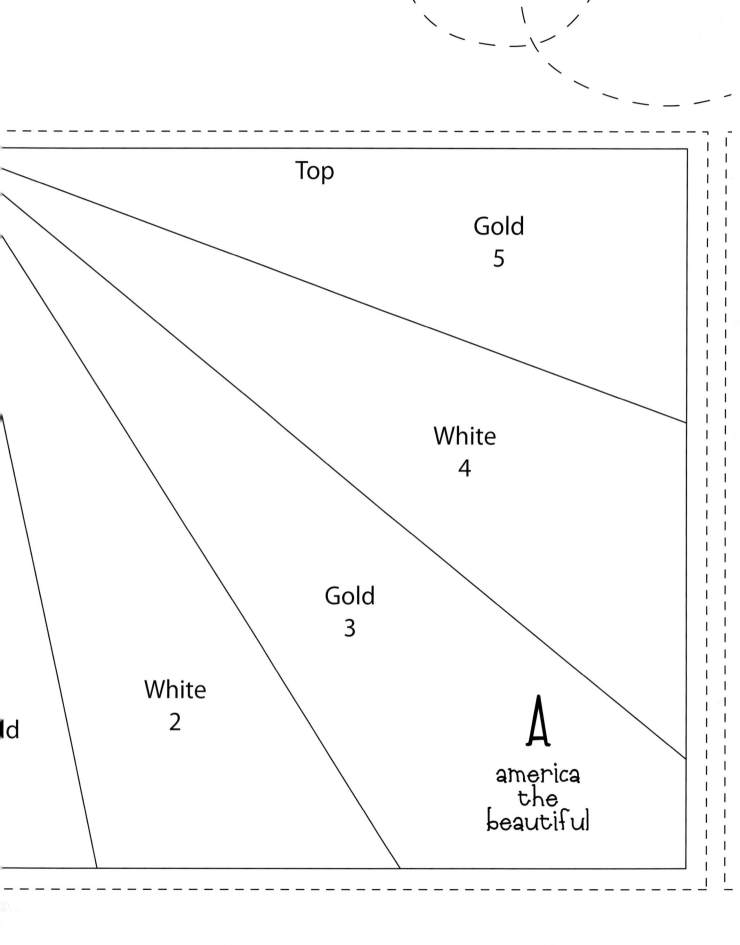

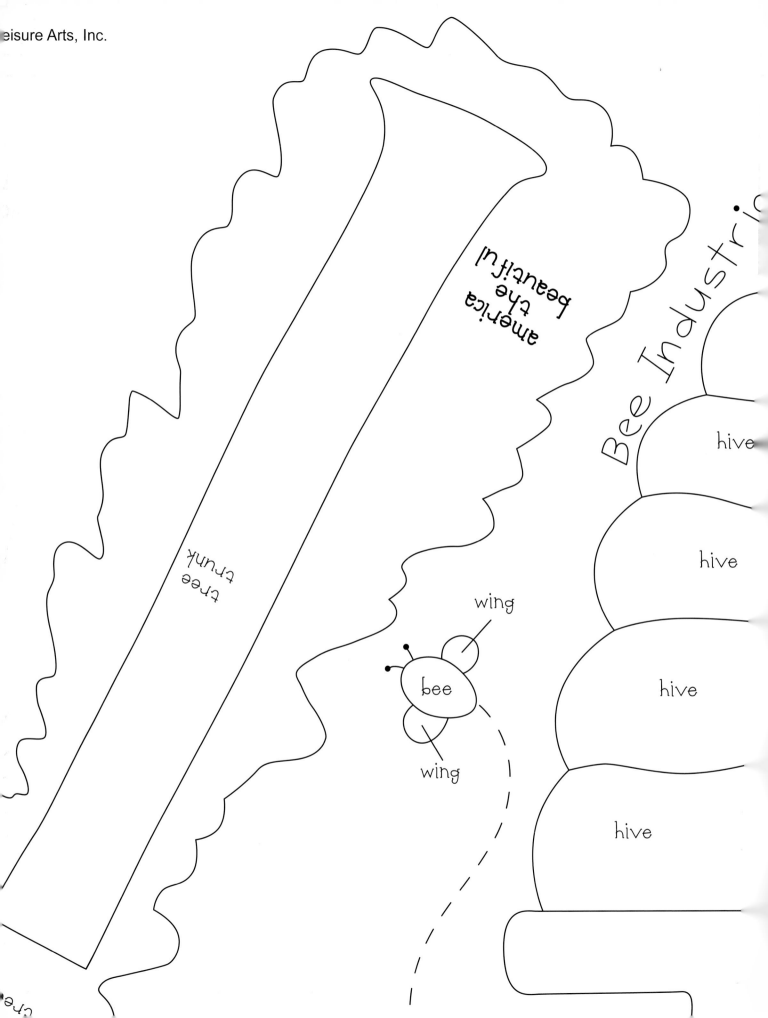

Bee Industri

hive

hive

hive

hive

wing

bee

wing

tree trunk

america the beautiful

pumpkin leaf

pumpkin stem

large hay

robe

straw

manger

large pumpkin

pumpkin
stem

pumpkin leaf

autumn
prairie

tall pumpkin

pumpkin
leaf

pumpkin
stem

pumpkin
leaf

small round pumpkin

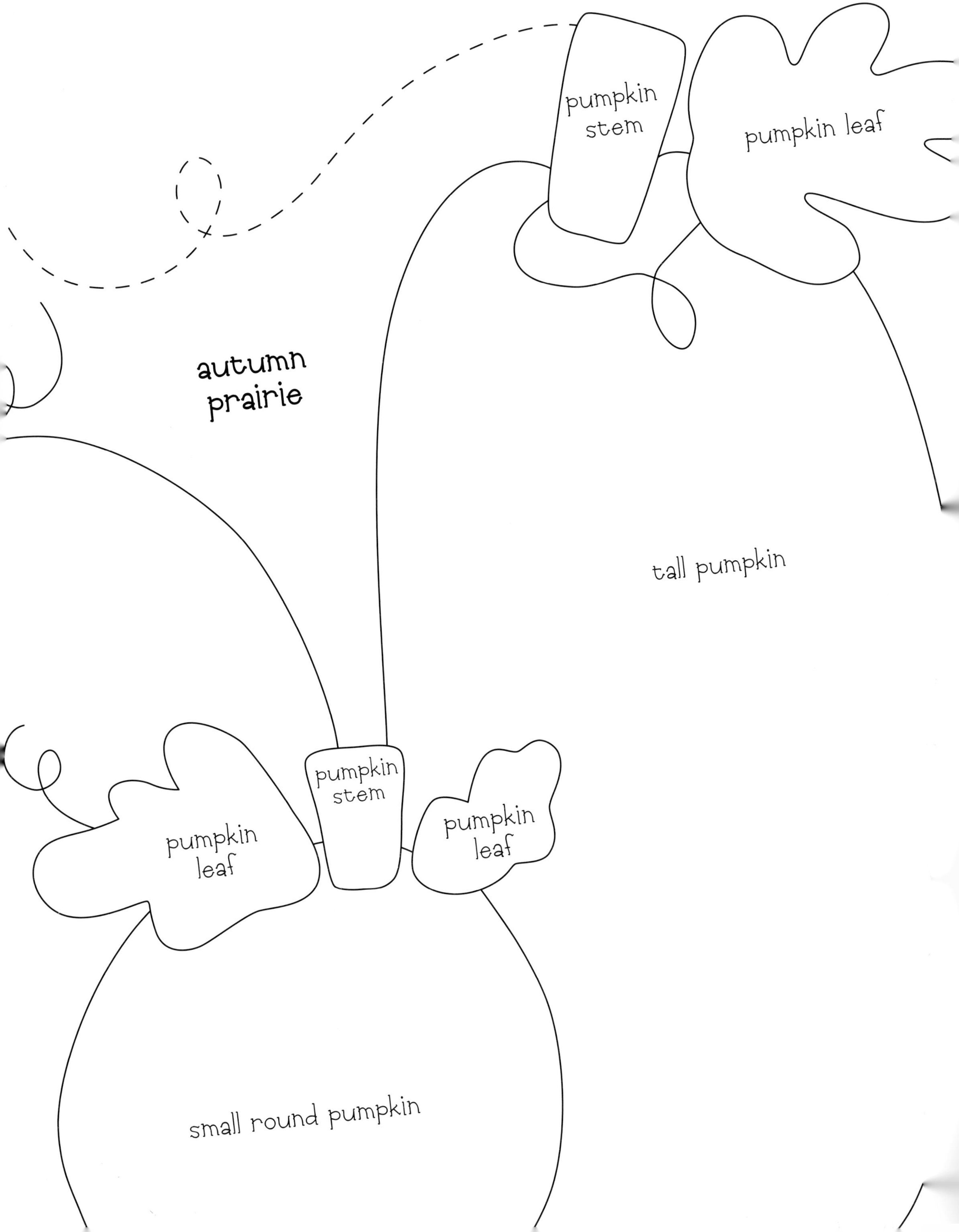

tree
trunk

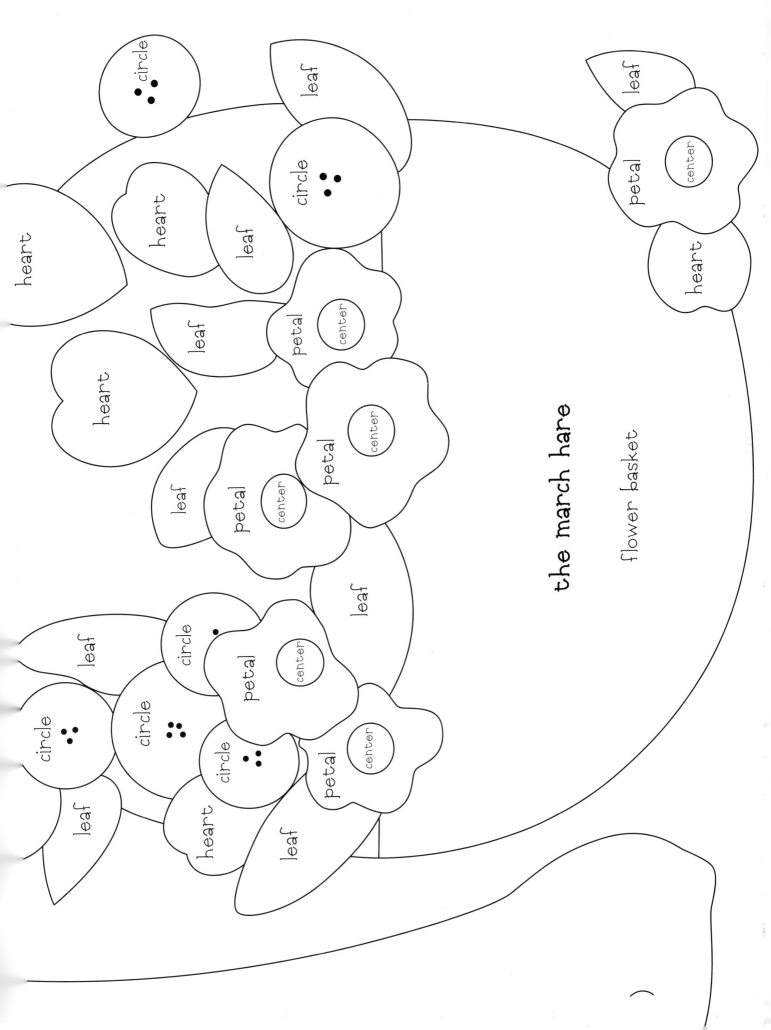

the march hare

flower basket

star

field

flag

star

star

star

star

bud

July

August

leaf

leaf

sunflower

center

leaf

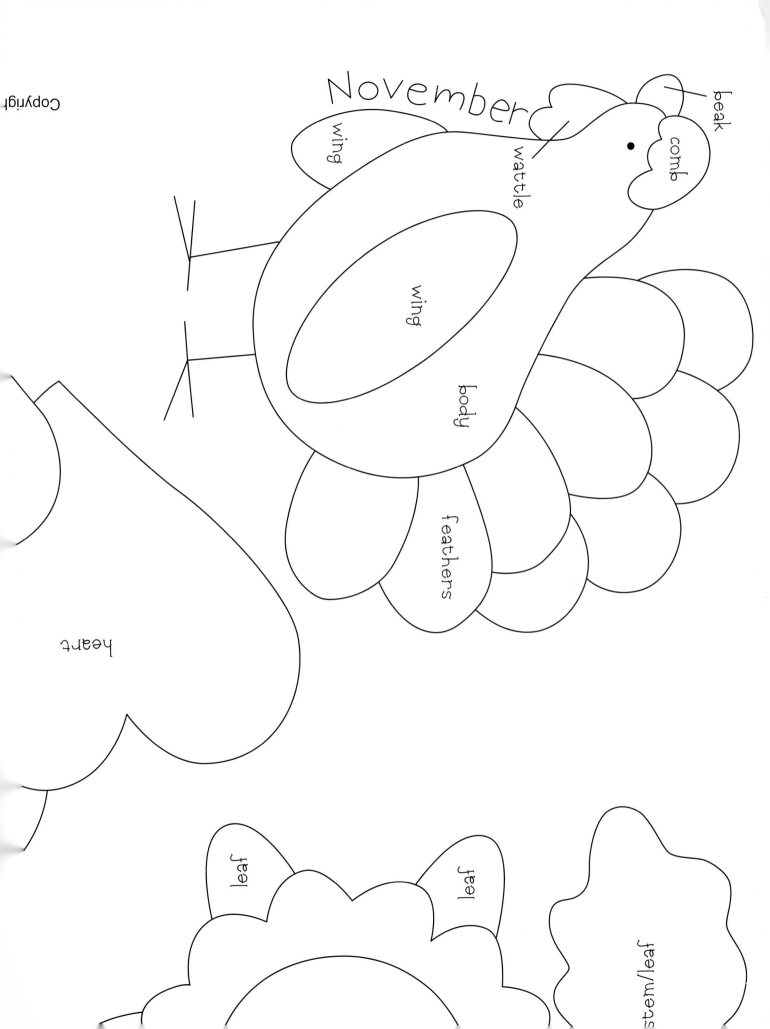

November

beak

comb

wattle

wing

wing

body

feathers

heart

leaf

leaf

stem/leaf

the march hare

hare

let it snow banner

america the beautiful

THIS LAND SH

A LAND OF LIB

FROM SEA TO SHINING

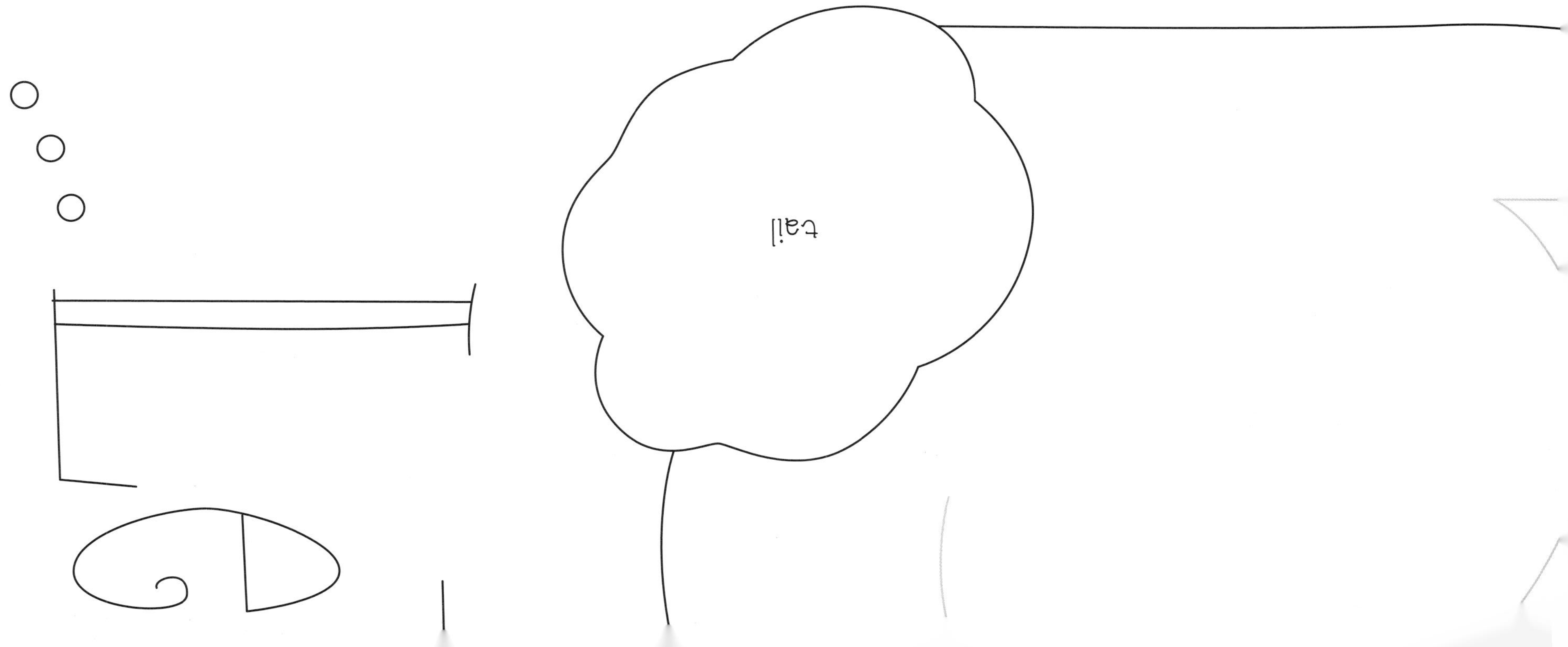

tail

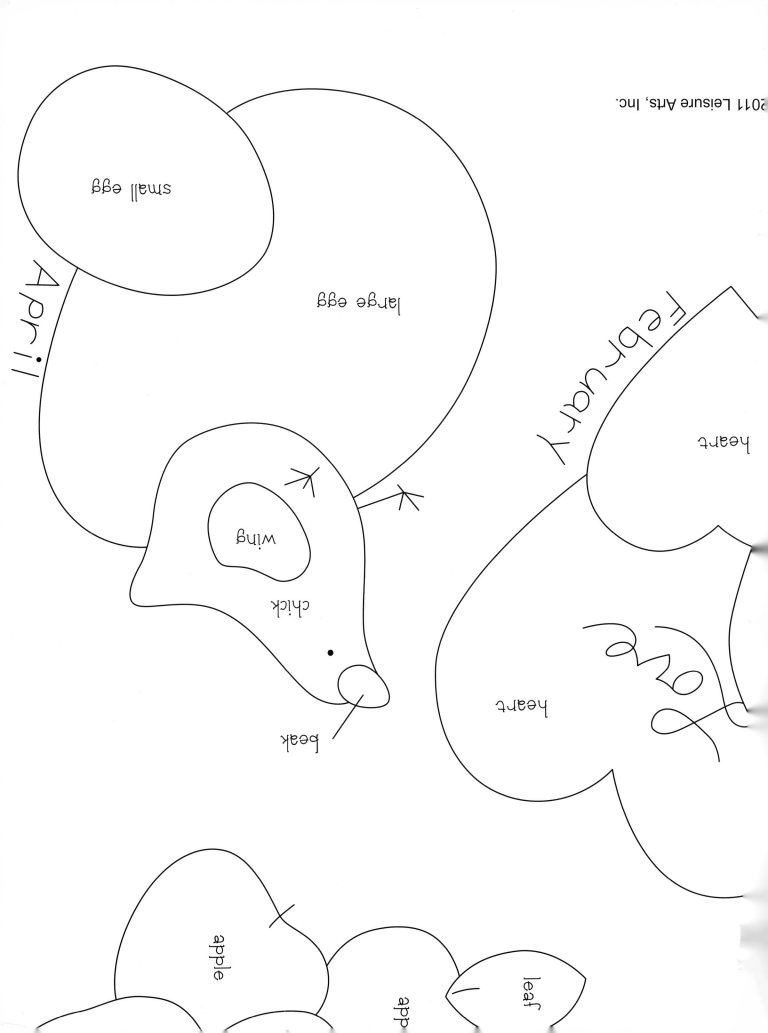

small egg

large egg

April

February

heart

heart

love

wing

chick

beak

apple

apple

leaf

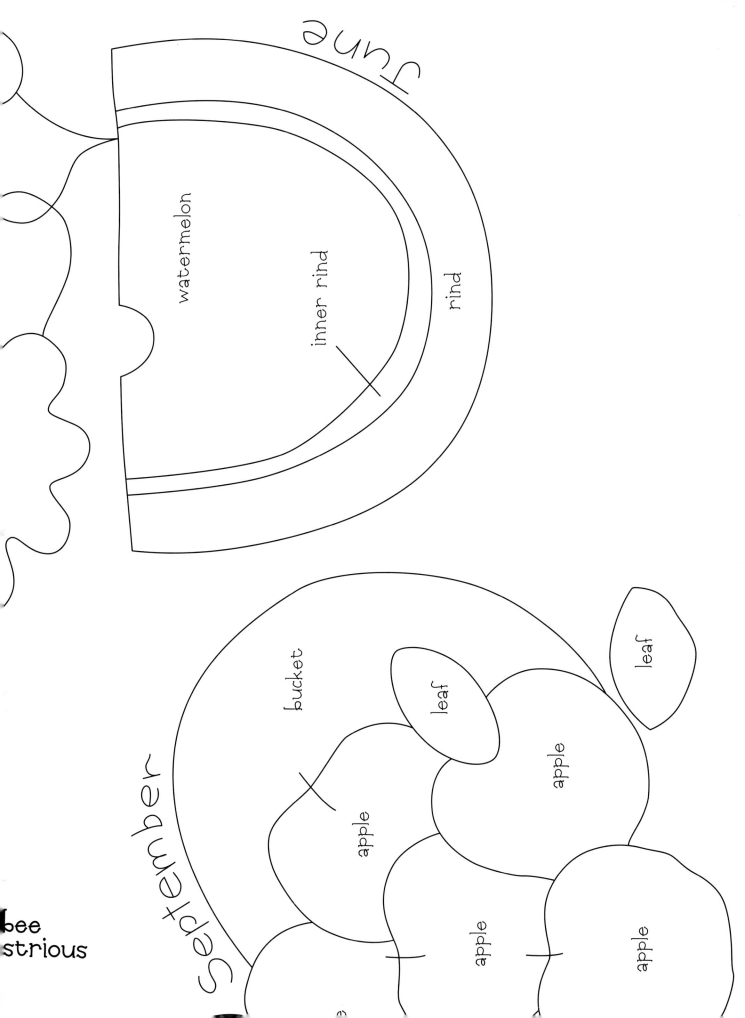

June

watermelon

inner rind

rind

September

bucket

leaf

leaf

apple

apple

apple

apple

bee

strious

egg basket handle

large
egg

small
egg

grass

the march hare

egg basket

the march hare

Come Spring!

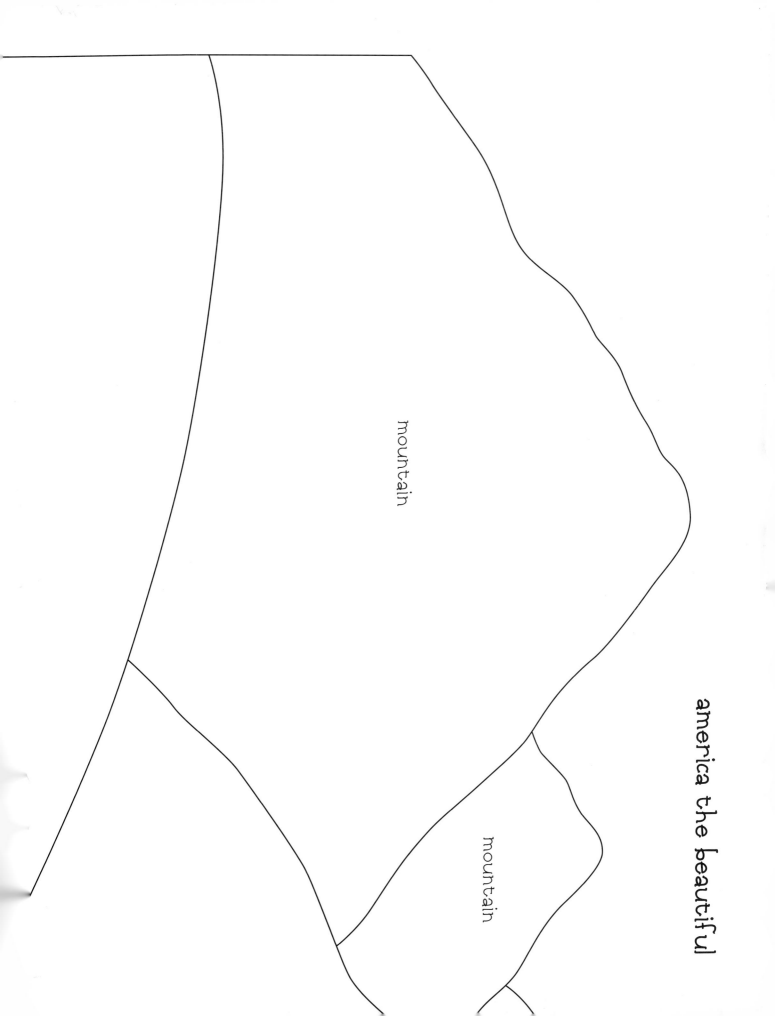

mountain

mountain

america the beautiful

scarf

nose

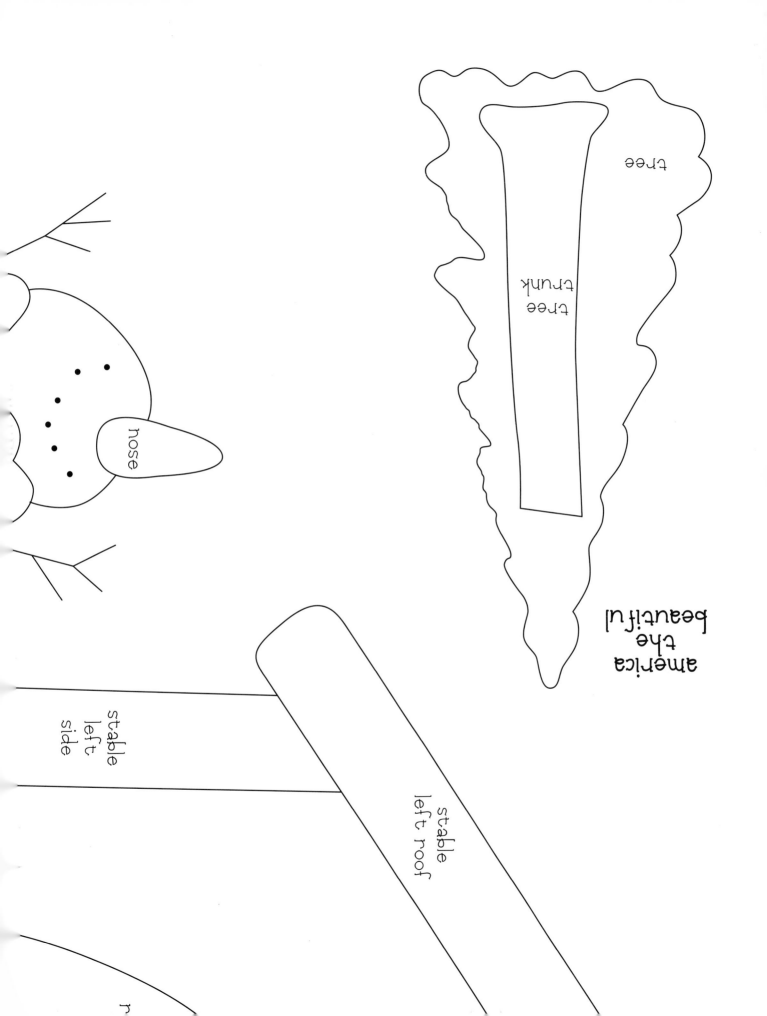

nose

tree

tree trunk

america
the
beautiful

stable
left
side

stable
left roof

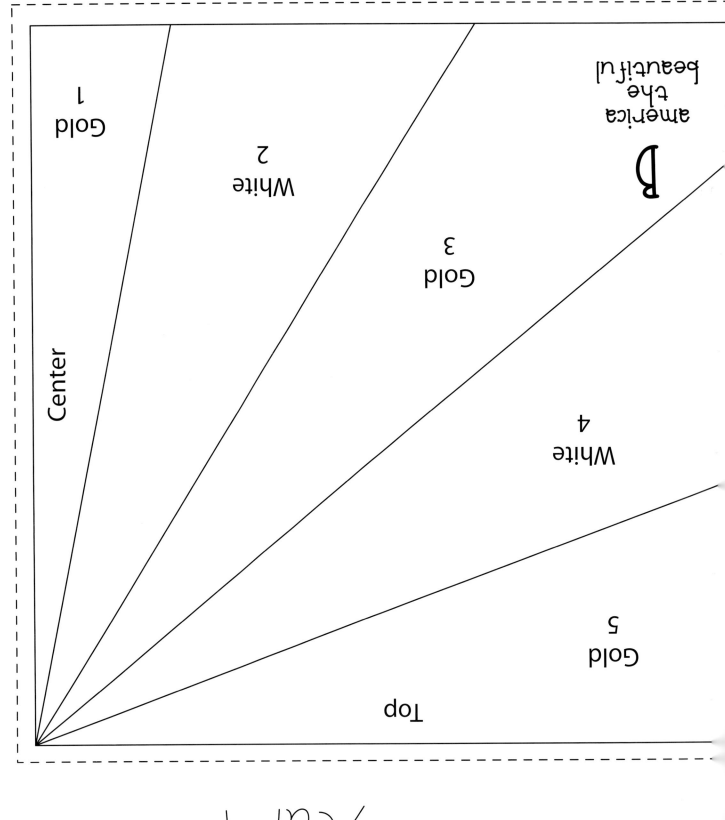

Gold 1

White 2

Gold 3

America the beautiful

B

White 4

Gold 5

Center

Top

...All year 'Round

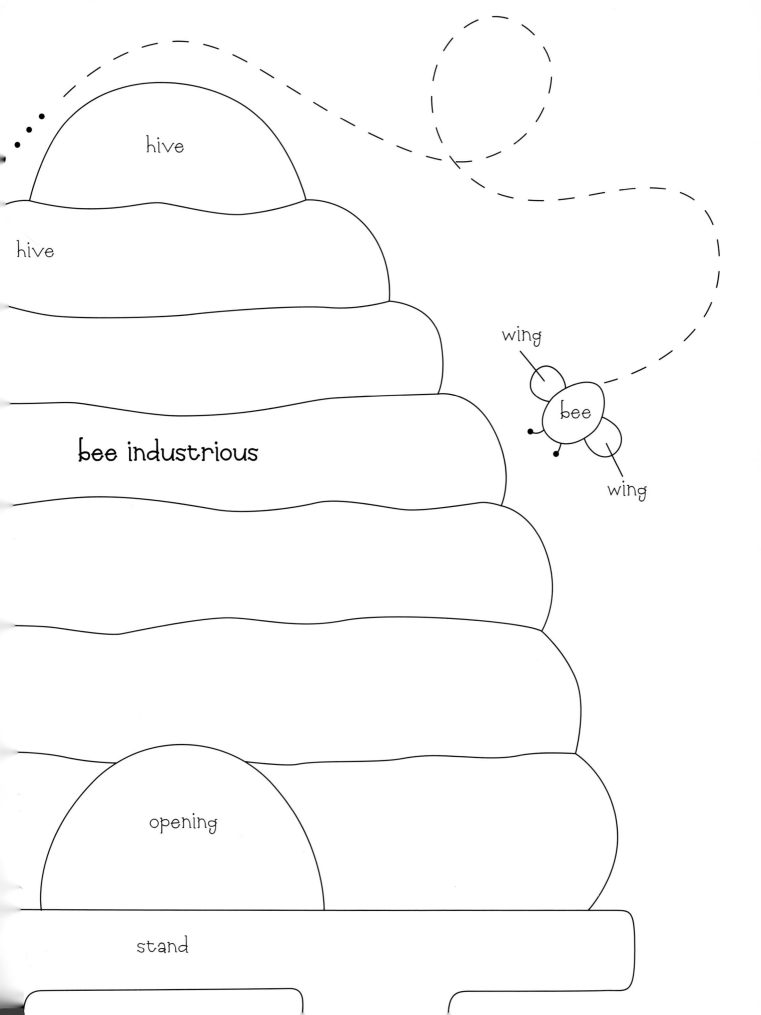

hive

hive

bee industrious

wing

bee

wing

opening

stand

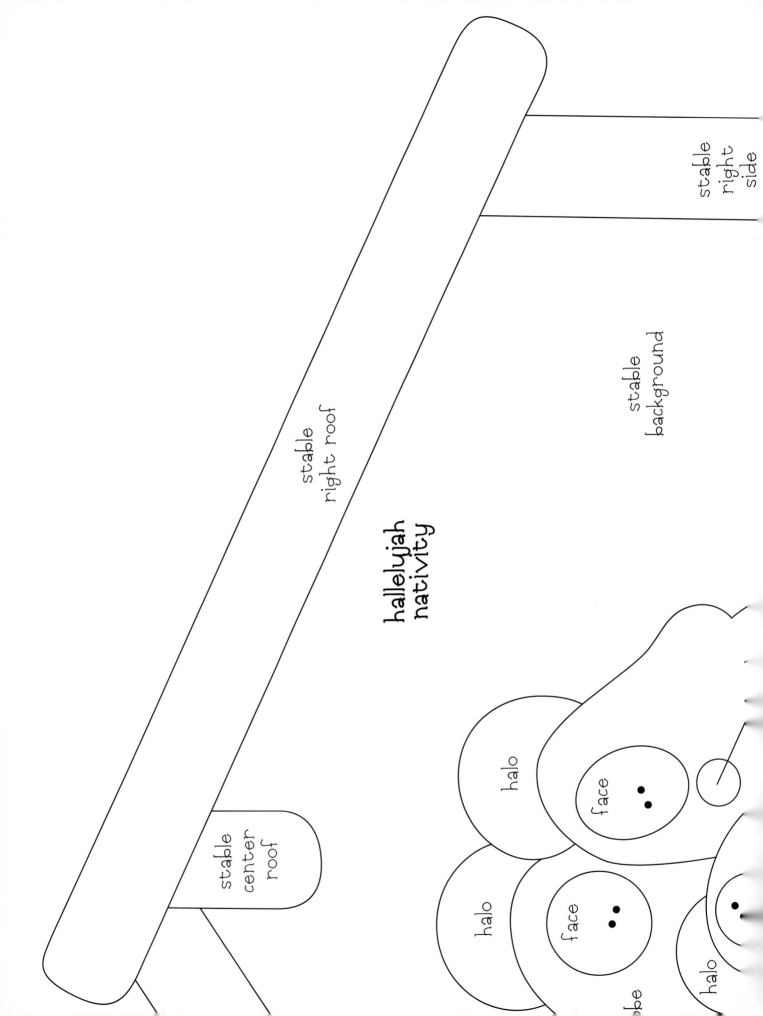

stable right side

stable right roof

stable background

hallelujah nativity

stable center roof

halo

halo

face

face

halo

halo

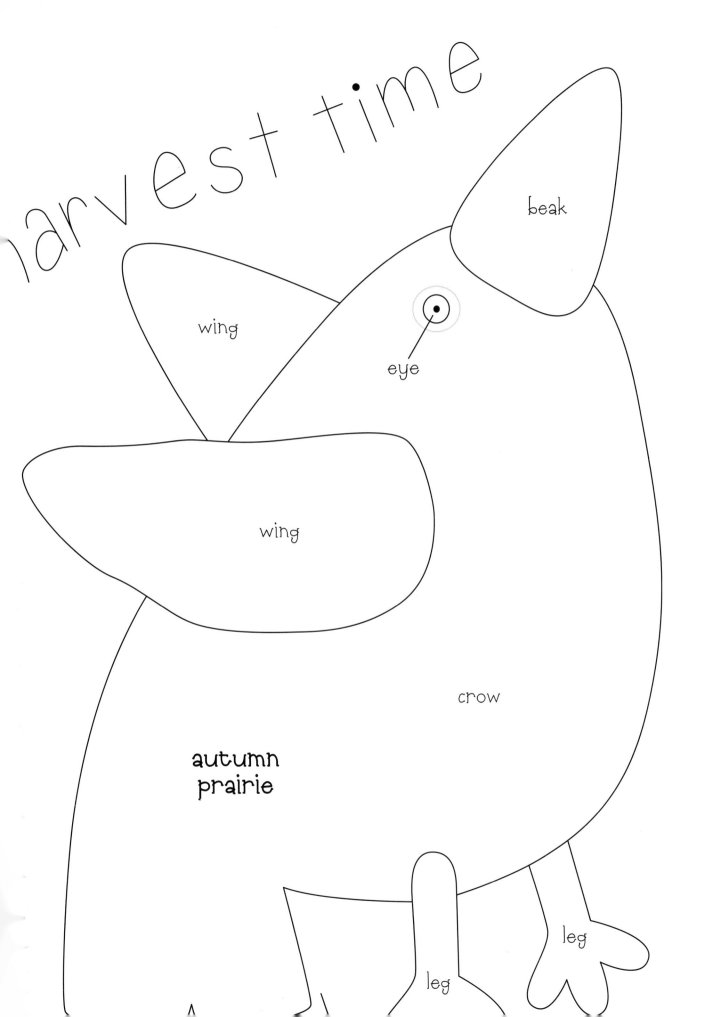

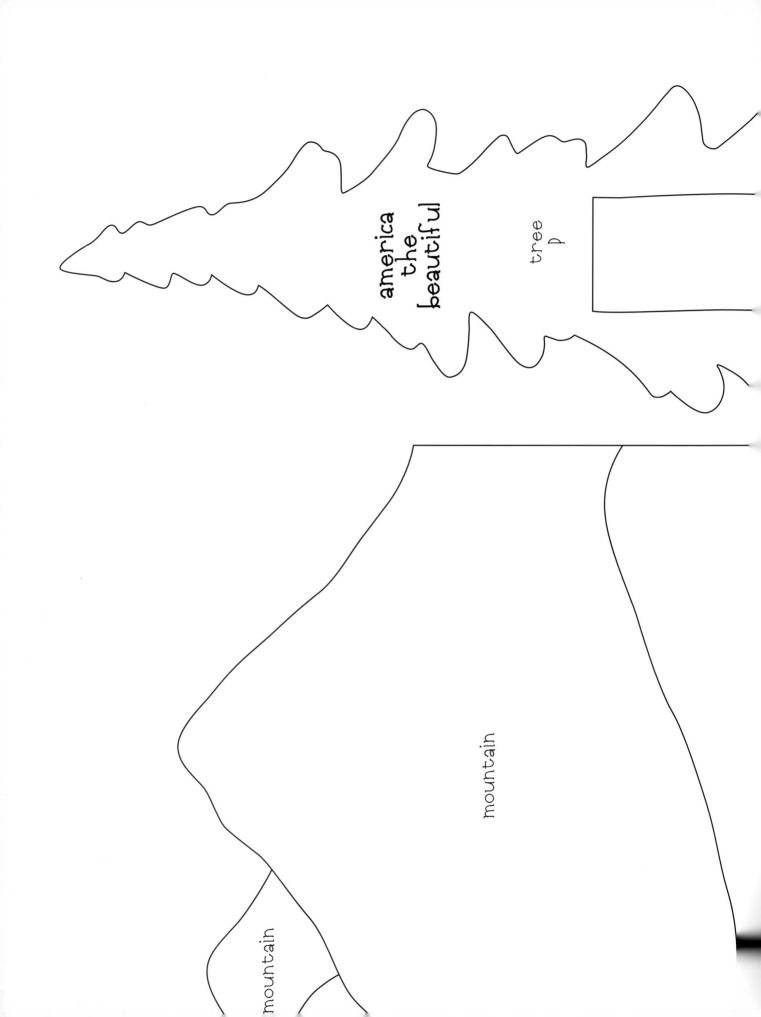

america
the
beautiful

tree
p

mountain

mountain

assembling the quilt top

Refer to photo, page 25, for placement.

1. Sew **Sun Block**, **Flag Block**, and **Landscape Block** together to complete **quilt top center**.
2. Matching centers and corners, sew **side**, and then **top/bottom borders** to quilt top center to make **quilt top**.
3. Arrange, fuse, and Blanket Stitch **tree trunks** and **trees** to quilt top.

completing the quilt

1. Follow **Quilting**, page 50, to mark, layer, and quilt as desired. Our quilt is hand quilted with a Running Stitch outlining all blocks and large appliqué shapes.
2. If desired, follow **Adding A Hanging Sleeve**, page 52, to add a hanging sleeve.
3. Follow **Binding**, page 52, to bind quilt using **binding strips**.

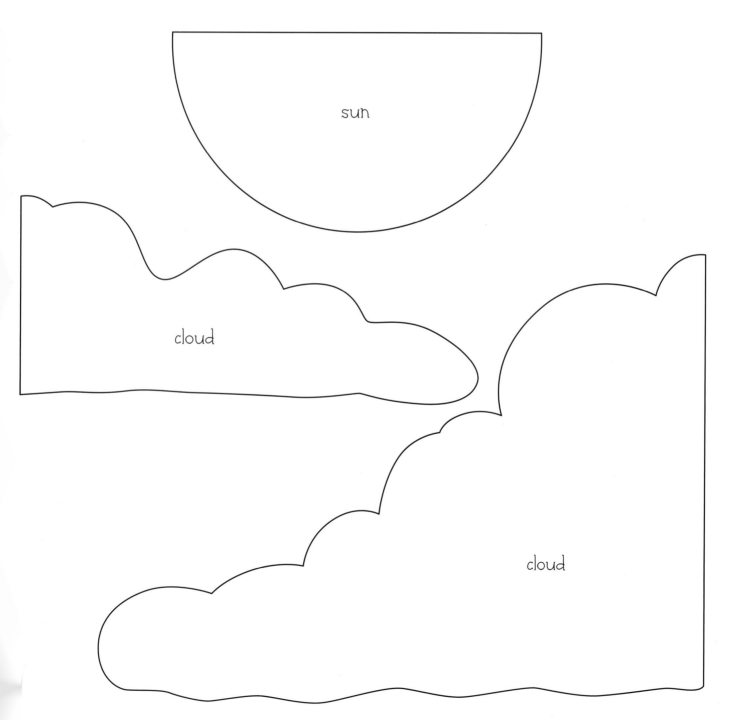

autumn

quilt size: 35" x 35" (89 cm x 89 cm)

fabric requirements

Yardage is based on 43"/44" (109 cm/112 cm) wide fabric. **Note**: *A fat quarter measures approximately 18" x 22" (46 cm x 56 cm) and a fat eighth measures approximately 11" x 18" (28 cm x 46 cm).*

- 1 fat quarter *each* of 8 tan prints for backgrounds
- $^1/_2$ yd (46 cm) of tan print for outer border
- $^3/_8$ yd (34 cm) of dark tan print for binding
- 1 fat eighth *each* of 4 autumn-colored prints for leaf blocks
- 1 fat eighth of light purple print for checkerboard unit
- $^3/_8$ yd (34 cm) of purple print for inner border
- 1 fat eighth of black print for checkerboard unit
- 1 fat eighth *each* of gold, rust, orange, and black prints for appliqués
- Assorted scrap fabrics for Prairie Points and appliqués
- $2^1/_2$ yds (2.3 m) of fabric for backing

You will also need:

- 43" x 43" (109 cm x 109 cm) square of batting
- Black #8 pearl cotton
- Green, red, yellow, lavender, and orange embroidery floss
- 48 brown $^3/_8$" (9 mm) buttons
- 1 bumblebee button

prairie

harvest time

cutting the pieces

Follow **Rotary Cutting**, *page 45, to cut fabric. Cut all strips across the selvage-to-selvage width of the fabric. Measurements given for* **backgrounds** *are exact. You may wish to cut these pieces 1" larger on all sides to allow for fraying and take up during appliqué and embroidery. Trim pieces to sizes given after all stitching is completed. All measurements include ¼" seam allowances.*

From tan print fat quarters:
- Cut 1 **pumpkin background** 16½" x 12½".
- Cut 1 **crow background** 10" x 12½".
- Cut 1 **wreath background** 7" x 7".
- Cut 1 **acorn background** 7" x 6".
- Cut 4 *sets* of 2 **small squares** 2½" x 2½".
- Cut 4 *sets* of 2 **large squares** 3" x 3".

From tan print:
- Cut 2 **side outer borders** 3¼" x 29".
- Cut 2 **top/bottom outer borders** 3¼" x 34½".

From dark tan print:
- Cut 4 **binding strips** 2½" wide.

From autumn-colored print fat eighths:
- Cut 4 *sets* of 3 **small squares** 2½" x 2½".
- Cut 4 *sets* of 2 **large squares** 3" x 3".

From light purple print fat eighth:
- Cut 3 **strips** 1½" x 18".

From purple print fabric:
- Cut 2 **side inner borders** 2¾" x 24½".
- Cut 2 **top/bottom inner borders** 2¾" x 29".

From black print fat eighth:
- Cut 3 **strips** 1½" x 18".

From assorted scrap fabrics:
- Cut 48 **Prairie Point squares** 3½" x 3½".

cutting the appliqués

Follow **Fusible Appliqué**, *page 47, to use patterns on page 35 and pattern insert.*

From gold print fat eighth:
- Cut 1 **large pumpkin**.

From rust print fat eighth:
- Cut 1 **tall pumpkin**.

From orange print fat eighth:
- Cut 1 **small pumpkin**.
- Cut 1 of *each* **leg**.

From black print fat eighth:
- Cut 1 **crow**.

From assorted scrap fabrics:
- Cut 1 of *each* **pumpkin stem**.
- Cut 1 of *each* **pumpkin leaf**.
- Cut 1 of *each* **wing**.
- Cut 1 **beak**.
- Cut 1 **eye**.
- Cut 1 of *each* **acorn**.
- Cut 1 of *each* **acorn cap**.
- Cut 1 of *each* **acorn stem**.
- Cut 1 of *each* **wreath leaf**.

making the blocks and units

Follow **Machine Piecing** and **Pressing**, *page 46. Use a ¼" seam allowance. Refer to* **Blanket Stitch Appliqué**, *pages 48-49, for Hand or Machine Appliqué techniques. Refer to* **Transferring Patterns**, *page 49, to transfer embroidery details and* **Hand Stitches**, *pages 54-56, for embroidery stitches.*

leaf block

For each Leaf Block, you will need 1 set of 2 tan small squares and 2 tan large squares and 1 set of 3 autumn-colored small squares and 2 large squares.

1. Draw a diagonal line on wrong side of each tan **large square**. With right sides together, place 1 tan large square on top of an autumn-colored **large square**. Stitch seam ¼" from each side of drawn line (**Fig. 1**).

Fig. 1

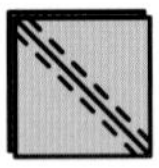

2. Cut along drawn line and press open to make 2 **Triangle Squares**. Make 4 Triangle Squares. Trim Triangle Squares to 2$\frac{1}{2}$" x 2$\frac{1}{2}$".

Triangle Squares (make 4)

3. Sew 4 Triangle-Squares, 3 autumn-colored **small squares** and 2 tan **small squares** together. Use 6 strands of embroidery floss to add a Backstitch stem to complete **Leaf Block**. Make 4 Leaf Blocks.

Leaf Block (make 4)

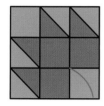

checkerboard unit

1. Sew 3 light purple **strips** and 3 black **strips** together to make **Strip Set**. Cut across Strip Set at 1$\frac{1}{2}$" intervals to make **Unit 1**. Make 8 Unit 1's.

Unit 1
(make 8)

Strip Set

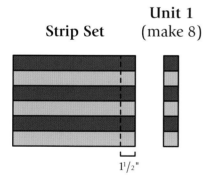

1$\frac{1}{2}$"

2. Matching short edges, sew 4 Unit 1's together to make a **Row**. Make 2 Rows. Sew Rows together to complete **Checkerboard Unit**.

Row (make 2)

Checkerboard Unit

pumpkin block

1. Arrange, fuse, and Blanket Stitch **appliqué shapes** to **pumpkin background**.
2. Transfer embroidery details to pumpkin background. Use black pearl cotton to work a Running Stitch bee trail. Chain Stitch tendrils using 3 strands of green embroidery floss.

Pumpkin Block

crow block

1. Arrange, fuse, and Blanket Stitch **appliqué shapes** to **crow background**.
2. Transfer embroidery details to crow background. Use black pearl cotton to work Backstitch wording, dotting the "i" with a French Knot. Backstitch a circle around eye using 3 strands of red embroidery floss and add a black pearl cotton French Knot pupil.

Crow Block

33

1. Arrange, fuse, and Blanket Stitch **appliqué shapes** to **acorn background**.

Acorn Block

1. Arrange, fuse, and Blanket Stitch **appliqué shapes** to **wreath background**.
2. Transfer heart embroidery design to center of wreath. Work Lazy Daisy leaves using 2 strands of green embroidery floss and French Knot flowers using 2 strands of lavender embroidery floss. Work a Running Stitch heart inside the wreath using 2 strands of orange embroidery floss.

Wreath Block

assembling the quilt top

Refer to photo, page 31, for placement.

1. Sew 4 **Leaf Blocks**, **Checkerboard Unit**, **Pumpkin Block**, **Crow Block**, **Wreath Block**, and **Acorn Block** together to complete **quilt top center**.
2. Matching centers and corners, sew **side inner borders**, and then **top/bottom inner borders** to quilt top center. Place a mark at the center of each edge of quilt top center.

3. For each **Prairie Point**, fold 1 **Prairie Point square** in half diagonally with wrong sides together and then fold in half again; press. Make 48 Prairie Points.

Prairie Point (make 48)

4. Matching right sides, raw edges, and tucking single-fold edge of one point into the open side of adjacent point, evenly space 12 Prairie Points on each side of quilt top center. Points should overlap by $1/4$" at each corner (**Fig. 2**). When folded up, points should meet exactly at corners (**Fig. 3**). Pin and then baste Prairie Points in place.

Fig. 2

Fig. 3

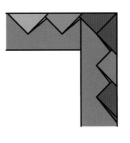
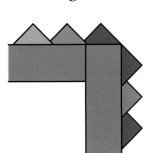

5. Matching centers and corners, sew **side**, and then **top/bottom outer borders** to quilt top center to complete **quilt top**.

completing the quilt

1. Follow **Quilting**, page 50, to mark, layer, and quilt as desired. Our quilt is hand quilted with a Running Stitch outlining the blocks and large appliqué shapes. There is an X through the center of each group of 4 squares in the checkerboard unit.
2. If desired, follow **Adding A Hanging Sleeve** page 52, to add a hanging sleeve.
3. Follow **Binding**, page 52, to bind quilt using **binding strips**.
4. Using black pearl cotton and stitching through all layers, sew a brown button to the point of each Prairie Point and the bee button to the Pumpkin Block.

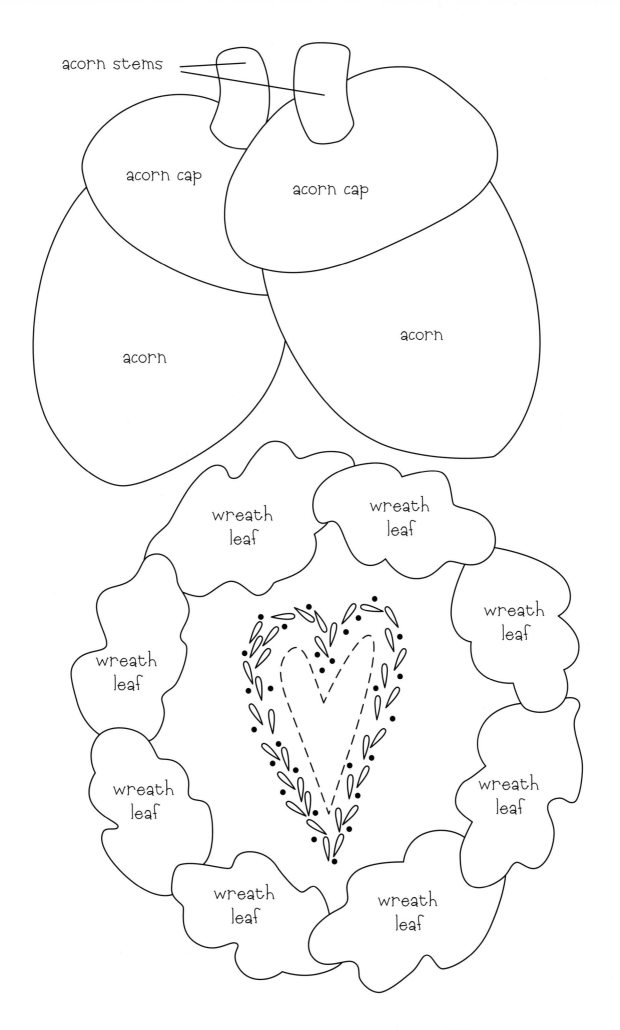

acorn stems

acorn cap

acorn cap

acorn

acorn

wreath leaf

wreath leaf

wreath leaf

wreath leaf

wreath leaf

wreath leaf

wreath leaf

wreath leaf

hallelujah nativity

quilt size: 23" x 41" (58 cm x 104 cm)

fabric requirements

Yardage is based on 43"/44" (109 cm/112 cm) wide fabric. **Note**: *A fat quarter measures approximately 18" x 22" (46 cm x 56 cm) and a fat eighth measures approximately 11" x 18" (28 cm x 46 cm).*

- 1 fat quarter *each* of 3 dark blue prints for sky
- 1 fat quarter of navy print for checkered inner border
- 1 fat quarter of cream print for checkered inner border
- 1 fat eighth of green print for grass
- $5^1/_2$" x $5^1/_2$" (14 cm x 14 cm) square of *each* of 3 green prints for animal backgrounds
- 1 fat eighth of gold print for pieced star
- $^1/_2$ yd (46 cm) of red stripe for outer border
- $^3/_8$ yd (34 cm) of tan print for binding
- 1 fat quarter *each* of 1 brown and 1 gold print for stable
- Assorted scrap fabrics for appliqués
- $1^1/_4$ yds (1.1 m) of fabric for backing

You will also need:

- 31" x 49" (79 cm x 124 cm) rectangle of batting
- Black and white #8 pearl cotton

cutting the pieces

*Follow **Rotary Cutting**, page 45, to cut fabric. Cut border strips across the selvage-to-selvage width of the fabric. Measurements given for **backgrounds** are exact. You may wish to cut these pieces 1" larger on all sides to allow for fraying and take up during appliqué and embroidery. Trim pieces to sizes given after all stitching is completed. All measurements include $1/4$" seam allowances.*

From 1 dark blue print fat quarter:
- Cut 1 **star background** $7^1/_2$" x $8^1/_2$".
- Cut 8 **small squares** $1^3/_4$" x $1^3/_4$".
- Cut 1 **medium square** $2^1/_2$" x $2^1/_2$".
- Cut 2 **rectangles** $2^1/_2$" x 4".
- Cut 1 **large square** 4" x 4".

From remaining 2 dark blue fat quarters:
- Cut 1 **angel background** $7^1/_2$" x $15^1/_2$".
- Cut 1 **nativity background** $10^1/_2$" x $15^1/_2$".

From navy print fat quarter:
- Cut 6 **strips** $1^1/_2$" x 22".

From cream print fat quarter:
- Cut 6 **strips** $1^1/_2$" x 22".

From green print fat eighth:
- Cut 1 **grass strip** $3^1/_2$" x $15^1/_2$".

From gold print fat eighth:
- Cut 4 **small rectangles** $1^3/_4$" x $2^1/_2$".
- Cut 4 **medium rectangles** $1^3/_4$" x 4".
- Cut 1 **center square** 3" x 3".

From red stripe:
- Cut 2 **side borders** 3" x 44", pieced as necessary.
- Cut 2 **top/bottom borders** 3" x 26".

From tan print:
- Cut 4 **binding strips** $2^1/_2$" wide.

cutting the appliqués

*Follow **Fusible Appliqué**, page 47, to use patterns on pages 42-44 and pattern inserts.*

From gold print fat quarter:
- Cut 1 **stable background**.

From brown print fat quarter:
- Cut 1 **stable left side**.
- Cut 1 **stable right side**.
- Cut 1 **stable left roof**.
- Cut 1 **stable right roof**.
- Cut 1 **stable center roof**.

From assorted scrap fabrics:
- Cut 1 of *each* **wing**.
- Cut 1 **angel gown**.
- Cut 1 of *each* **halo**.
- Cut 1 of *each* **face**.
- Cut 1 **banner**.
- Cut 1 of *each* **star**.
- Cut 1 **baby gown**.
- Cut 1 **hand**.
- Cut 1 of *each* **robe**.
- Cut 1 **manger**.
- Cut 1 **straw**.
- Cut 1 **large hay** and 1 **small hay**.
- Cut 1 **donkey**.
- Cut 1 **blanket**.
- Cut 1 **cow**.
- Cut 1 **cow face**.
- Cut 1 **cow spot**.
- Cut 1 **sheep fleece**.
- Cut 1 **sheep face**.
- Cut 1 of *each* **sheep leg**.

making the blocks

Follow **Machine Piecing** and **Pressing**, page 46.
Use a ¹/₄" seam allowance. Refer to **Blanket Stitch
Appliqué**, pages 48-49, for Hand or Machine
Appliqué techniques. Refer to **Transferring Patterns**,
page 49, to transfer embroidery details and **Hand
Stitches**, pages 54-56, for embroidery stitches.

angel block

1. Arrange, fuse, and Blanket Stitch **appliqué
   shapes** to **angel background**.
2. Transfer embroidery details to angel
   background. Use black pearl cotton to work
   Backstitch wording, a French Knot dot over
   the "j", and French Knot eyes.

Angel Block

star block

1. For **Appliquéd Star**, arrange, fuse, and
   Blanket Stitch **appliqué shapes** to **star
   background**.

Appliquéd Star

2. For **Pieced Star**, place 1 dark blue **small
   square** on one corner of 1 gold **medium
   rectangle** and stitch diagonally across small
   square from upper right to lower left. Trim
   ¹/₄" from stitching line (**Fig. 1**) press open to
   make **Unit 1**. Make 2 Unit 1's.

Fig. 1

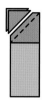

Unit 1
(make 2)

3. Stitching from upper left to bottom right
   across small square (**Fig. 2**), repeat Step 2
   to make 2 **Unit 2's**.

Fig. 2

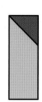

Unit 2
(make 2)

4. Repeat Steps 2 and 3 using dark blue small
   squares and gold **small rectangles** to make
   2 **Unit 3's** and 2 **Unit 4's**.

Unit 3
(make 2)

Unit 4
(make 2)

5. Sew 1 dark blue **medium square**, 1 **Unit 3**,
   1 **Unit 4** and 1 dark blue **rectangle** to
   complete **Row 1**.

Row 1

6. Sew 1 Unit 1 and 1 Unit 2 together to make **Unit 5**. Sew 1 Unit 3 and 1 Unit 4 together to make **Unit 6**. Sew Unit 5, gold **center square**, and Unit 6 together to complete **Row 2**.

Unit 5   **Unit 6**

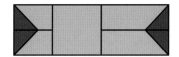

Row 2

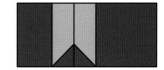

7. Sew 1 dark blue **rectangle**, 1 **Unit 1**, 1 **Unit 2,** and 1 dark blue **large square** together to complete **Row 3**.

Row 3

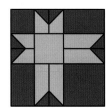

8. Sew Rows together to complete **Pieced Star**.

Pieced Star

9. Sew Pieced Star and Appliqué Star together to complete **Star Block**.

Star Block

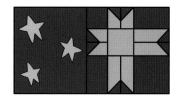

1. Arrange, fuse, and Blanket Stitch **stable background**, **stable sides**, and **stable roof** to **nativity background**. Sew **grass strip** to bottom edge of nativity background.
2. Arrange, fuse, and Blanket Stitch **appliqué shapes** to nativity background.
3. Use black pearl cotton to work French Knot eyes to complete **Stable Unit**.

Stable Unit

4. To make **Donkey Unit** arrange, fuse, and Blanket Stitch **appliqué shapes** to 1 green **animal background square**. Work a French Knot eye with black pearl cotton.

Donkey Unit

5. To make **Cow Unit**, arrange, fuse, and Blanket Stitch **appliqué shapes** to 1 green **animal background square**. Work French Knot eyes with black pearl cotton.

Cow Unit

6. To make **Sheep Unit**, arrange, fuse, and Blanket Stitch **appliqué shapes** to 1 green **animal background square**. Work French Knot eyes with white pearl cotton.

Sheep Unit

7. Sew **Donkey**, **Cow**, and **Sheep Units** together to make **Animal Unit**. Sew Animal Unit to the bottom edge of Stable Unit to complete **Nativity Block**.

Animal Unit

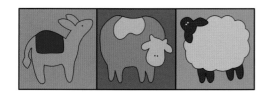

Nativity Block

assembling the quilt top

Refer to photo, page 37, for placement.

1. Sew **Angel Block**, **Star Block**, and **Nativity Block** together to make **quilt top center**.
2. For inner borders, alternate colors and sew 6 **navy** and 6 **cream strips** together to make **Strip Set**. Cut across Strip Set at $1^1/_2$" intervals to make **Unit 1**. Make 10 Unit 1's.

Strip Set   **Unit 1**

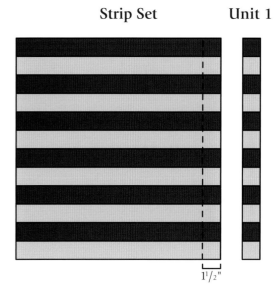

$1^1/_2$"

3. Sew 2 Unit 1's together to make **top/bottom inner** border. Remove a total of 7 squares from top/bottom inner border (17 squares remaining). Make 2 top/bottom inner borders.

Top/bottom inner border (make 2)

4. Sew 3 Unit 1's together to make **side inner border**. Remove a total of 3 squares from side inner border (33 squares remaining) Make 2 side inner borders.

Side inner border (make 2)

5. Matching centers and corners, sew **side** then **top/bottom inner borders** to quilt top center.
6. Mark the center of each edge of quilt top. Mark center of 1 long edge of each border.

7. Matching center marks and raw edges, pin border to center of quilt top edge. Beginning at center of border, measure $^1/_2$ the width of the quilt top in both directions and mark. Match marks on border with corners of quilt top and pin. Easing in any fullness, pin border to quilt top between center and corners. Sew border to quilt top, beginning and ending seams exactly $^1/_4$" from each corner of quilt top and backstitching at beginning and end of stitching (**Fig. 3**).

Fig. 3

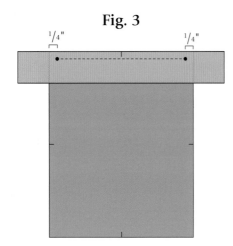

8. Repeat Step 7 to sew 1 border to bottom edge of quilt top. Fold and pin ends of top and bottom borders out of the way, and then sew remaining borders to side edges of quilt top.

9. Fold 1 corner of quilt top diagonally with right sides together and matching edges. Use ruler to mark stitching line as shown in **Fig. 4**. Pin borders together along drawn line. Sew on drawn line, backstitching at beginning and end of stitching.

Fig. 4

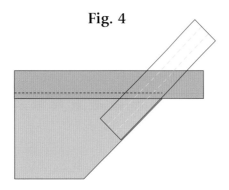

10. Turn mitered corner right side up. Check to make sure corner will lie flat with no gaps or puckers.
11. Trim seam allowance to $^1/_4$"; press to 1 side.
12. Repeat Steps 9-11 to miter each remaining corner.

completing the quilt

1. Follow **Quilting**, page 50, to mark, layer, and quilt as desired. Our quilt is hand quilted with a Running Stitch outlining the blocks and large appliqué shapes. There are Running Stitch lines radiating from manger.
2. If desired, follow **Adding A Hanging Sleeve**, page 52, to add a hanging sleeve.
3. Follow **Binding**, page 52, to bind quilt using **binding strips**.

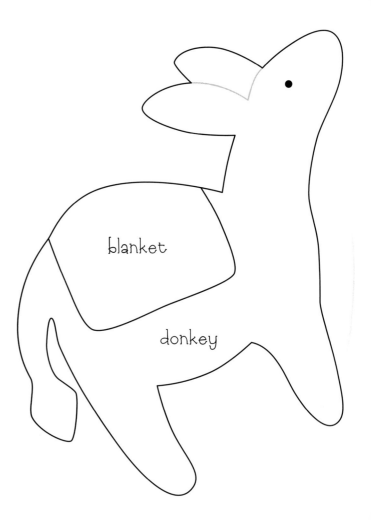

blanket

donkey

sheep face

sheep fleece

star

sheep legs

star

cow spot

cow

cow face

star

wing

Hallelujah

halo

face

angel gown

banner

wing

general instructions

To make your quilting easier and more enjoyable, we encourage you to carefully read all of the general instructions, study the color photographs, and familiarize yourself with the individual project instructions before beginning a project.

fabrics

selecting fabrics

Choose high-quality, medium-weight 100% cotton fabrics. All-cotton fabrics hold a crease better, fray less, and are easier to quilt than cotton/polyester blends.

Yardage requirements listed for each project are based on 43"/44" wide fabric with a "usable" width of 40" after shrinkage and trimming selvages. Actual usable width will probably vary slightly from fabric to fabric. Our recommended yardage lengths should be adequate for occasional re-squaring of fabric when many cuts are required.

preparing fabrics

We recommend that all fabrics be washed, dried, and pressed before cutting. If fabrics are not pre-washed, washing the finished quilt will cause shrinkage and give it a more "antique" look and feel. Bright and dark colors, which may run, should always be washed before cutting. After washing and drying fabric, fold lengthwise with wrong sides together and matching selvages.

rotary cutting

Rotary cutting has brought speed and accuracy to quiltmaking by allowing quilters to easily cut strips of fabric and then cut those strips into smaller pieces.

- Place fabric on work surface with fold closest to you.

- Cut all strips from the selvage-to-selvage width of the fabric unless otherwise indicated in project instructions.

- Square left edge of fabric using rotary cutter and rulers (**Figs. 1-2**).

Fig. 1	**Fig. 2**

- To cut each strip required for a project, place ruler over cut edge of fabric, aligning desired marking on ruler with cut edge; make cut (**Fig. 3**).

Fig. 3

45

- When cutting several strips from a single piece of fabric, it is important to make sure that cuts remain at a perfect right angle to the fold; square fabric as needed.

Machine piecing

Precise cutting, followed by accurate piecing, will ensure that all pieces of quilt top fit together well.

- Set sewing machine stitch length for approximately 11 stitches per inch.

- Use neutral-colored general-purpose sewing thread (not quilting thread) in needle and in bobbin.

- An accurate $1/4$" seam allowance is *essential*. Presser feet that are $1/4$" wide are available for most sewing machines.

- When piecing, always place pieces right sides together and match raw edges; pin if necessary.

- Chain piecing saves time and will usually result in more accurate piecing.

- Trim away points of seam allowances that extend beyond edges of sewn pieces.

sewing strip sets

When there are several strips to assemble into a strip set, first sew strips together into pairs, then sew pairs together to form strip set. To help avoid distortion, sew seams in opposite directions (**Fig. 4**).

Fig. 4

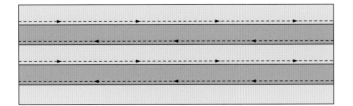

sewing across seam intersections

When sewing across intersection of two seams, place pieces right sides together and match seams exactly, making sure seam allowances are pressed in opposite directions (**Fig. 5**).

Fig. 5

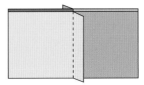

sewing sharp points

To ensure sharp points when joining triangular or diagonal pieces, stitch across the center of the "X" (shown in pink) formed on wrong side by previous seams (**Fig. 6**).

Fig. 6

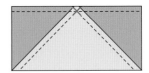

pressing

- Use steam iron set on "Cotton" for all pressing.

- Press after sewing each seam.

- Seam allowances are almost always pressed to one side, usually toward darker fabric. However, to reduce bulk it may occasionally be necessary to press seam allowances toward the lighter fabric or even to press them open.

- To prevent dark fabric seam allowance from showing through light fabric, trim darker seam allowance slightly narrower than lighter seam allowance.

- To press long seams, such as those in long strip sets, without curving or other distortion, lay strips across width of the ironing board.

fusible appliqué

types of patterns

You'll need to look at each design and decide which pieces are layered and which overlap one another. The techniques for making patterns for the different situations vary just a bit.

For pieces that are layered, no underlap is necessary. A pattern will be needed for the base and for each separate appliqué that will be layered on the base. A good example of this is the April Block from Bee Industrious, page 3. You need one pattern for the large egg (the base) and separate patterns for the chick, wing, beak, and small egg.

April Block

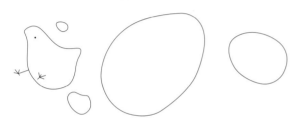

For pieces that overlap, you will need to add a $1/8$" to $1/4$" underlap to the bottom piece(s). A good example of this is the February Block from Bee Industrious, page 3. The hearts are cut $1/8$" to $1/4$" larger (shown in grey) where they are overlapped by another heart.

February Block

making patterns

When using fusible web, appliqué patterns need to be reversed from the way they appear on the finished project.

To reverse patterns for overlapped pieces, place, tracing paper over the design. Trace each portion of the design separately, adding underlaps as necessary; turn paper over.

To reverse patterns for pieces without underlaps, place tracing paper over the design. Trace each portion of the design separately; turn paper over.

preparing fusible appliqués

White or light-colored fabrics may need to be lined with fusible interfacing before applying fusible web to prevent darker fabrics from showing through.

1. Place paper-backed fusible web, paper side up, over appliqué pattern. Trace pattern onto paper side of web with pencil as many times as indicated in project instructions for a single fabric.
2. Follow manufacturer's instructions to fuse traced patterns to wrong side of fabrics. Do not remove paper backing. (Note: Some pieces may be given as measurements, such as a 2" x 4" rectangle, instead of drawn patterns. Fuse web to wrong side of fabrics indicated for these pieces.)
3. Use scissors to cut out appliqué pieces along traced lines; use rotary cutting equipment to cut out appliqué pieces given as measurements. Remove paper backing from all pieces.

Blanket stitch appliqué

Models were appliquéd using a Hand Blanket Stitch, page 49. If you prefer to appliqué by machine, follow Machine Blanket Stitch Appliqué, below.

machine blanket stitch appliqué

Some sewing machines feature a Blanket Stitch. Refer to your owner's manual for machine set-up. If your machine does not have this stitch, try other decorative stitches until you are satisfied with the look.

1. Thread sewing machine and bobbin with black 100% cotton thread in desired weight.
2. Attach an open-toe presser foot. Select far right needle position and needle down (if your machine has these features).
3. If desired, pin a commercial stabilizer to wrong side of background fabric or spray wrong side of background fabric with starch to stabilize.
4. Bring bobbin thread to the top of the fabric by lowering then raising the needle, bringing up the bobbin thread loop. Pull the loop all the way to the surface.
5. Begin by stitching 5 or 6 stitches in place (drop feed dogs or set stitch length at 0), or use your machine's lock stitch feature, if equipped, to anchor thread. Return setting to selected Blanket Stitch.
6. Most of the Blanket Stitch should be done on the appliqué with the right edges of the stitch falling at the very outside edge of the appliqué. Stitch over all exposed raw edges of appliqué pieces.

7. *(Note: Dots on Figs. 7-11 indicate where to leave needle in fabric when pivoting.)* Always stopping with needle down in background fabric, refer to **Fig. 7** to stitch outside points like tips of leaves. Stop one stitch short of point. Raise presser foot. Pivot project slightly, lower presser foot, and make on angled **Stitch 1**. Take next stitch, stop at point, and pivot so **Stitch 2** will be perpendicular to point. Pivot slightly to make **Stitch 3**. Continue stitching.

Fig. 7

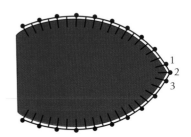

8. For outside corners (**Fig. 8**), stitch to corner, stopping with needle in background fabric. Raise presser foot. Pivot project, lower presser foot, and take an angled stitch. Raise presser foot. Pivot project, lower presser foot and stitch adjacent side.

Fig. 8

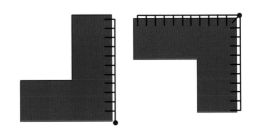

9. For inside corners (**Fig. 9**), stitch to the corner, taking the last bite at corner and stopping with the needle down in background fabric. Raise presser foot. Pivot project, lower presser foot, and take an angled stitch. Raise presser foot. Pivot project, lower presser foot and stitch adjacent side.

Fig. 9

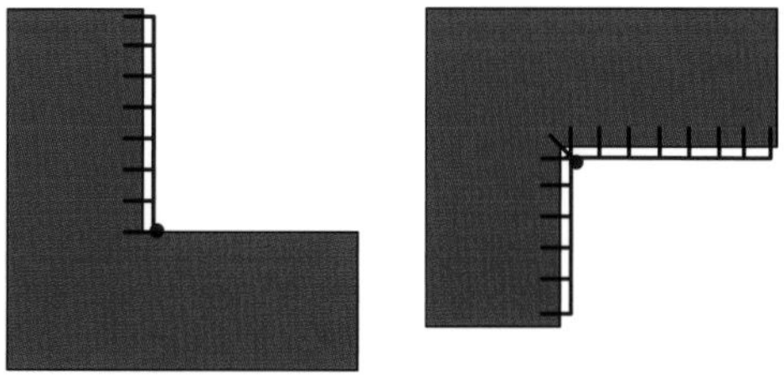

10. When stitching outside curves (**Fig. 10**), stop with needle down in background fabric. Raise presser foot and pivot project as needed. Lower presser foot and continue stitching, pivoting as often as necessary to follow curve. Small circles may require pivoting between each stitch.

Fig. 10

11. When stitching inside curves (**Fig. 11**), stop with needle down in background fabric. Raise presser foot and pivot project as needed. Lower presser foot and continue stitching, pivoting as often as necessary to follow curve.

Fig. 11

12. When stopping stitching, use a lock stitch to sew 5 or 6 stitches in place or use a needle to pull threads to wrong side of background fabric; knot, then trim ends.

13. Carefully tear away stabilizer, if used.

hand blanket stitch appliqué
Spacing stitches approximately ¹/₈" apart, work **Blanket Stitches**, page 55, around the edges of each appliqué shape using black pearl cotton. Refer to **Figs. 7-11**, pages 48-49, for stitch placement when turning corners and stitching around curves.

transferring patterns
If the fabric is sheer enough, place the pattern under the fabric and trace the embroidery details with water-soluble fabric pen. Otherwise, trace the pattern onto tissue paper and tape it and the fabric to a sunny window; then, trace the embroidery details onto the fabric. Embroider the design.

quilting

Quilting holds the three layers (top, batting, and backing) of the quilt together and can be done by hand or machine. Because marking, layering, and quilting are interrelated and may be done in different orders depending on circumstances, please read entire **Quilting** *section, pages 50–52, before beginning project.*

types of quilting designs

In the Ditch Quilting

Quilting along seamlines or along edges of appliquéd pieces is called "in the ditch" quilting. This type of quilting should be done on side **opposite** seam allowance and does not have to be marked.

Outline Quilting

Quilting a consistent distance, usually $1/4$", from seam or appliqué is called "outline" quilting. Outline quilting may be marked, or $1/4$" masking tape may be placed along seamlines for quilting guide. (Do not leave tape on quilt longer than necessary, since it may leave an adhesive residue.)

preparing the backing

To allow for slight shifting of quilt top during quilting, backing should be approximately 4" larger on all sides. Yardage requirements listed for quilt backings are calculated for 43"/44"w fabric. To piece a backing using 43"/44"w fabric, use the following instructions.

1. Measure length and width of quilt top; add 8" to each measurement.
2. If determined width is less than 40", cut backing fabric the measurements determined in Step 1.

3. If determined width is between 40" and 79", cut backing fabric into two lengths slightly longer than determined *length* measurement. Trim selvages. Place lengths with right sides facing and sew long edges together, forming tube (**Fig. 12**). Match seams and press along one fold (**Fig. 13**). Cut along pressed fold to form single piece (**Fig. 14**).

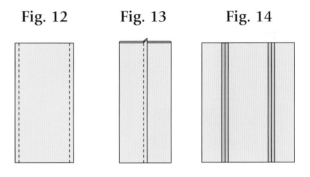

| Fig. 12 | Fig. 13 | Fig. 14 |

4. Trim backing to size determined in Step 1; press seam allowances open.

choosing the batting

The appropriate batting will make quilting easier. For fine hand quilting, choose low-loft batting. All cotton or cotton/polyester blend battings work well for machine quilting because the cotton helps "grip" quilt layers. If quilt is to be tied, a high-loft batting, sometimes called extra-loft or fat batting, may be used to make quilt "fluffy."

Types of batting include cotton, polyester, wool, cotton/polyester blend, cotton/wool blend, and silk.

When selecting batting, refer to package labels for characteristics and care instructions. Cut batting same size as prepared backing.

assembling the quilt

1. Examine wrong side of quilt top closely; trim any seam allowances and clip any threads that may show through front of the quilt. Press quilt top, being careful not to "set" any marked quilting lines.

2. Place backing *wrong* side up on flat surface. Use masking tape to tape edges of backing to surface. Place batting on top of backing fabric. Smooth batting gently, being careful not to stretch or tear. Center quilt top *right* side up on batting.

3. If hand quilting, begin in center and work toward outer edges to hand baste all layers together. Use long stitches and place basting lines approximately 4" apart (**Fig. 15**). Smooth fullness or wrinkles toward outer edges.

Fig. 15

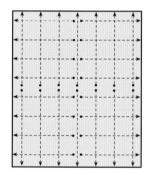

hand quilting

The quilting stitch is a basic running stitch that forms a broken line on quilt top and backing. Stitches on quilt top and backing should be straight and equal in length.

1. Secure center of quilt in hoop or frame. Check quilt top and backing to make sure they are smooth. To help prevent puckers, always begin quilting in the center of quilt and work toward outside edges.

2. Thread needle with 18" - 20" length of quilting thread; knot one end. Using thimble, insert needle into quilt top and batting approximately 1/2" from quilting line. Bring needle up on quilting line (**Fig. 16**); when knot catches on quilt top, give thread a quick, short pull to "pop" knot through fabric into batting (**Fig. 17**).

Fig. 16

Fig. 17

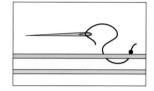

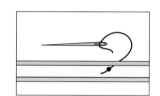

3. Holding needle with sewing hand and placing other hand underneath quilt, use thimble to push tip of needle down through all layers. As soon as needle touches finger underneath, use that finger to push tip of needle only back up through layers to top of quilt. (The amount of needle showing above fabric determines length of quilting stitch.) Referring to **Fig. 18**, rock needle up and down, taking three to six stitches before bringing needle and thread completely through layers. Check back of quilt to make sure stitches are going through all layers. If necessary, make one stitch at a time when quilting through seam allowances or along curves and corners.

Fig. 18

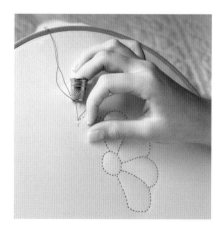

4. At end of thread, knot thread close to fabric and "pop" knot into batting; clip thread close to fabric.

5. Move hoop as often as necessary. Thread may be left dangling and picked up again after returning to that part of quilt.

adding a hanging sleeve

Attaching a hanging sleeve to back of wall hanging or quilt before the binding is added allows project to be displayed on wall.

1. Measure width of quilt top edge and subtract 1". Cut piece of fabric 7"w by determined measurement.

2. Press short edges of fabric piece $^1/_4$" to wrong side; press edges $^1/_4$" to wrong side again and machine stitch in place.

3. Matching wrong sides, fold piece in half lengthwise to form tube.

4. Follow project instructions to sew binding to quilt top and to trim backing and batting. Before Blindstitching binding to backing, match raw edges and stitch hanging sleeve to center top edge on back of quilt.

5. Finish binding quilt, treating hanging sleeve as part of backing.

6. Blindstitch bottom of hanging sleeve to backing, taking care not to stitch through to front of quilt.

binding

Binding encloses the raw edges of quilt. Because of its stretchiness, bias binding works well for binding projects with curves or rounded corners and tends to lie smooth and flat in any given circumstance. Binding may also be cut from straight lengthwise or crosswise grain of fabric.

1. Beginning with one end near center on bottom edge of quilt, lay binding around quilt to make sure that seams in binding will not end up at a corner. Adjust placement if necessary. Matching raw edges of binding to raw edge of quilt top, pin binding to right side of quilt along one edge.

2. When you reach first corner, mark $^1/_4$" from corner of quilt top (**Fig. 19**).

Fig. 19

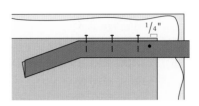

3. Beginning approximately 10" from end of binding and using $^1/_4$" seam allowance, sew binding to quilt, backstitching at beginning of stitching and at mark (**Fig. 20**). Lift needle out of fabric and clip thread.

Fig. 20

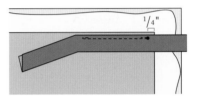

4. Fold binding as shown in **Figs. 21–22** and pin binding to adjacent side, matching raw edges. When you've reached the next corner, mark $^1/_4$" from edge of quilt top.

Fig. 21   **Fig. 22**

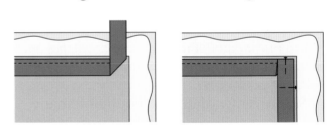

Backstitching at edge of quilt top, sew pinned binding to quilt (**Fig. 23**); backstitch at the next mark. Lift needle out of fabric and clip thread.

Fig. 23

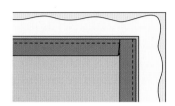

Continue sewing binding to quilt, stopping approximately 10" from starting point (**Fig. 24**).

Fig. 24

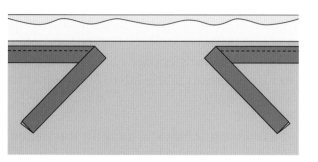

Bring beginning and end of binding to center of opening and fold each end back, leaving a ¹/₄" space between folds (**Fig. 25**). Finger press folds.

Fig. 25

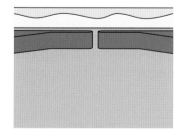

8. Unfold ends of binding and draw a line across wrong side in finger-pressed crease. Draw a line through the lengthwise pressed fold of binding at the same spot to create a cross mark. With edge of ruler at cross mark, line up 45° angle marking on ruler with one long side of binding. Draw a diagonal line from edge to edge. Repeat on remaining end, making sure that the two diagonal lines are angled the same way (**Fig. 26**).

Fig. 26

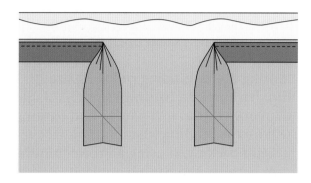

9. Matching right sides and diagonal lines, pin binding ends together at right angles (**Fig. 27**).

Fig. 27

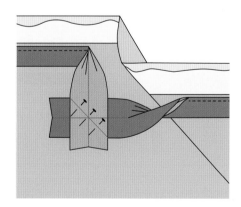

53

10. Machine stitch along diagonal line (**Fig. 28**), removing pins as you stitch.

Fig. 28

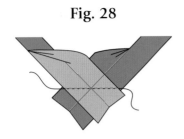

11. Lay binding against quilt to double check that it is correct length.
12. Trim binding ends, leaving ¹/₄" seam allowance; press seam open. Stitch binding to quilt.
13. If using 2¹/₂"w binding (finished size ¹/₂"), trim backing and batting a scant ¹/₄" larger than quilt top so that batting and backing will fill the binding when it is folded over to quilt backing. If using narrower binding, trim backing and batting even with edges of quilt top.
14. On one edge of quilt, fold binding over to quilt backing and pin pressed edge in place, covering stitching line (**Fig. 29**). On adjacent side, fold binding over, forming a mitered corner (**Fig. 30**). Repeat to pin remainder of binding in place.

Fig. 29   **Fig. 30**

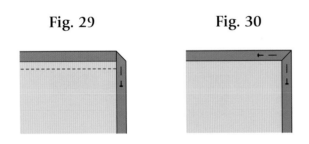

15. Blindstitch, page 55, binding to backing, taking care not to stitch through to front of quilt.

signing and dating your quilt

A completed quilt is a work of art and should be signed and dated. There are many different ways to do this and numerous books on the subject. The label should reflect the style of the quilt, the occasion or person for which it was made, and the quilter's own particular talents. Following are suggestions for recording the history of quilt or adding a sentiment for future generations.

- Embroider quilter's name, date, and any additional information on quilt top or backing. Matching floss, such as cream floss on white border, will leave a subtle record. Bright or contrasting floss will make the information stand out.

- Make label from muslin and use permanent marker to write information. Use different colored permanent markers to make label more decorative. Stitch label to back of quilt.

- Use photo-transfer paper to add image to white or cream fabric label. Stitch label to back of quilt.

- Piece an extra block from quilt top pattern to use as label. Add information with permanent fabric pen. Appliqué block to back of quilt.

- Write message on appliquéd design from quilt top. Attach appliqué to back of the quilt.

hand stitches
back stitch

Come up at 1, go down at 2, and come up at 3 (**Fig. 31**). Length of stitches may be varied as desired.

Fig. 31

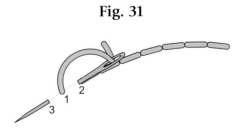

blanket stitch

Come up at 1, go down at 2, and come up at 3, keeping thread below point of needle (**Fig. 32**).

Fig. 32

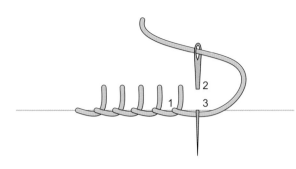

blind stitch

Come up at 1, go down at 2, and come up at 3 (**Fig. 33**). Length of stitches may be varied as desired.

Fig. 33

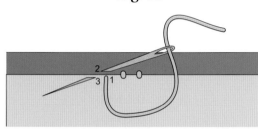

chain stitch

Come up at 1 and go down again at 1 to form a loop. Keeping loop below point of needle, come up at 2 and go down again at 2 to form second loop (**Fig. 34**). Continue making loops or "chain" until reaching end of line. Tack last loop (**Fig. 35**).

Fig. 34   **Fig. 35**

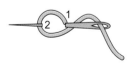   

french knot

Follow **Figs. 36–39** to complete French Knots. Come up at 1. Wrap thread once around needle and insert needle at 2, holding end of thread with non-stitching fingers. Tighten knot, then pull needle through, holding floss until it must be released.

Fig. 36   **Fig. 37**

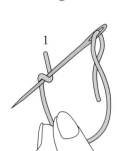   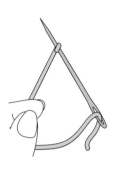

Fig. 38   **Fig. 39**

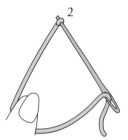   

lazy daisy stitch

Come up at 1 and go down again at 1 to form a loop. Come up at 2. Keeping loop below point of needle (**Fig. 40**), go down at 3 to anchor loop (**Fig. 41**).

Fig. 40   **Fig. 41**

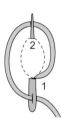   

running stitch

The running stitch consists of a series of straight stitches with the stitch length equal to the space between stitches. Come up at 1, go down at 2, and come up at 3. Go down at 4 (**Fig. 42**).

Fig. 42

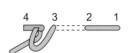

straight stitch

Come up at 1 and go down at 2 (**Fig. 43**). Length of stitches may be varied as desired.

Fig. 43

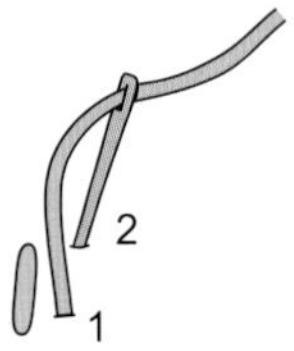

Metric Conversion Chart

Inches x 2.54 = centimeters (cm)	Yards x .9144 = meters (m)
Inches x 25.4 = millimeters (mm)	Yards x 91.44 = centimeters (cm)
Inches x .0254 = meters (m)	Centimeters x .3937 = inches (")
	Meters x 1.0936 = yards (yd)

Standard Equivalents

⅛"	3.2 mm	0.32 cm	⅛ yard	11.43 cm	0.11 m
¼"	6.35 mm	0.635 cm	¼ yard	22.86 cm	0.23 m
⅜"	9.5 mm	0.95 cm	⅜ yard	34.29 cm	0.34 m
½"	12.7 mm	1.27 cm	½ yard	45.72 cm	0.46 m
⅝"	15.9 mm	1.59 cm	⅝ yard	57.15 cm	0.57 m
¾"	19.1 mm	1.91 cm	¾ yard	68.58 cm	0.69 m
⅞"	22.2 mm	2.22 cm	⅞ yard	80 cm	0.8 m
1"	25.4 mm	2.54 cm	1 yard	91.44 cm	0.91 m

Production Team: Technical Editor – Lisa Lancaster; Technical Writer – Jean Lewis; Graphic Artists – Amy Temple, Becca Snider, Jacob Casleton, and Janie Marie Wright; Contributing Photographers – Mark Mathews and Ken West.

We have made every effort to ensure that these instructions are accurate and complete. We cannot, however, be responsible for human error, typographical mistakes, or variations in individual work.